Healing the Wounds of the Heart

15 Obstacles to Forgiveness and How to Overcome Them

by Olivier Clerc

Translated by Claire Webster

FINDHORN PRESS

Findhorn Press
One Park Street
Rochester, Vermont 05767
www.findhornpress.com

Findhorn Press is a division of Inner Traditions International

---

Disclaimer

The information in this book is given in good faith and intended for information only. Neither author nor publisher can be held liable by any person for any loss or damage whatsoever which may arise from the use of this book or any of the information therein.

Cataloging-in-Publication data for this title is available from the Library of Congress

ISBN 978-1-64411-598-5 (print)
ISBN 978-1-64411-599-2 (ebook)

Printed and bound in the United States by Versa Press, Inc.

10 9 8 7 6 5 4 3 2 1

Edited by Michael Hawkins
Text design and layout by Richard Crookes
Illustrations by Hung Ho Thanh
Cover image: iStock.com / stellalevi 483503126
This book was typeset in Adobe Garamond Pro

To send correspondence to the author of this book, mail a first-class letter to the author c/o Inner Traditions • Bear & Company, One Park Street, Rochester, VT 05767, USA, and we will forward the communication, or contact the author directly at **http://giftofforgiveness.olivierclerc.com**.

Table of Contents

Foreword

By Lewis Mehl-Madrona, M.D.,
author of *Coyote Wisdom*, *Narrative Medicine*
and *Healing the Mind through the Power of Story*

I met Olivier through his translating of my book, *Coyote Wisdom*, into French. I attended one of his forgiveness circles at a workshop in France and was deeply moved by the power of his simple ceremony.

I remember so well the intensity of progressing around a circle of people, looking each one in the eyes, and saying, "*Je te demande pardon* (I ask your forgiveness)." I remember the simultaneous hilarity and seriousness of asking forgiveness from the devil for all the things we have blamed upon him/her/it/them unfairly. The devil just isn't that powerful or ever present. The "devil," of course, is a metaphor for all those we have unfairly, incorrectly, or unjustly vilified for deeds that they did not commit, including random occurrences.

Each time I have done the circle of forgiveness with Olivier, it has been equally powerful. When I have done them in workshops, people are impressed with the depth and power and healing that can be achieved in a short period of time.

I have watched as Olivier has spread his circles of healing around the globe over the years and am deeply impressed by his mission of global forgiveness.

Definition of Forgiveness

Olivier reminds us that we need to know what we mean by forgiveness. He notes that mainstream Euro-American culture has but a vague understanding of what is meant by the word. This makes it hard for us to talk about forgiveness with each other or to consider forgiveness of others.

Here is Olivier's definition of forgiveness:

"Forgiveness – as we will consider it here – is indeed the healing, the curing of the heart's wounds. It's the balm that allows to cure them. It's the remedy to be applied to emotional poisons such as hatred, rancour and resentment. Without forgiveness, healing cannot be achieved. The wound has only been clumsily hidden. We hide it behind the stories we tell ourselves, so it's bound to reopen, and bleed again, at any time."

The research is clear – being angry and bitter and pessimistic and resentful are not conducive to good health. Feeling grateful, being optimistic, practicing radical acceptance, cultivating loving kindness are good for health.

The Deneh from northern New Mexico and Arizona believe that the evil we do on earth, the mean deeds, the hurtful remarks, the abusive acts, cannot enter spirit world and must remain on earth. Therefore they ceremonially close a hogan when someone dies, so that this evil, which they call *chinle*, cannot get out and adversely affect someone else.

Cultural differences in definitions also exist. For example, compared with U.S. citizens, Japanese people focus more on restoring harmony in a relationship after an offence; they emphasize the need to adjust and to decide to forgive. They put less emphasis on emotional forgiveness and attention to individuals in comparison with Americans. The high value placed on maintaining relationships in Japan leads to different understandings of forgiveness.

Native American Story of Forgiveness

When I ponder a question such as the nature of forgiveness, I look to traditional indigenous stories for help, for they contain the wisdom and the philosophy of many years. Grudges are not held long in traditional stories, though evil creatures are summarily dispatched. In one Abenaki-Penobscot story from where I live in Maine, Glooskap (the cultural hero of the Wabanaki people, sent by Creator to do the "finish carpentry" of creation since Creator was too far away), is annoyed by a strong wind that keeps him from paddling his canoe on the lake to where the ducks are swimming. He's hungry for duck, but he can't get to them.

He asks Grandmother Woodchuck, his mentor and advisor, from where comes the wind? She's reluctant to tell him, fearing that he has a scheme in mind. Finally, he convinces her to tell him who makes the wind. He learns about an eagle who perches on the tallest mountain and flaps its wings to make the wind. Glooskap climbs that mountain, and the wind is so fierce it blows off all his clothes and all his hair. Nevertheless, he makes it to the eagle and convinces it that there's a better mountain and that Glooskap can take it there. The eagle agrees and he wraps it into a rug and stuffs the eagle head-first into a hole on the other peak. He goes back to hunt duck, but everything has changed. The mosquitoes and the flies have taken over. Without the wind they can multiply aplenty. The lake has started to stink. The ducks are disgusted with the whole affair and have flown away.

Grandmother Woodchuck asked Glooskap what he has done. When he explains, she gives him a teaching about the balance of nature. Sheepishly, he climbs the mountain again, pulls the eagle out of the hole, and things return to normal. Revenge is never a consideration except perhaps in the sense of Glooskap's going after the wind-eagle so that he would have a better day for fishing and thinking that he knew enough to control it, which he didn't. Transgressions generally lead to teachings and not revenge.

In another Abenaki story, Glooskap enters a village which is in need of repairs. The people are nowhere to be scene. Glooskap finds them lying under maple trees, their mouths open, just letting the syrup drop down. In those days the syrup was thick and sweet and flowed all year long. The people had gotten fat and lazy from that constant supply of syrup. They've let their village deteriorate. Glooscap consults Creator and they decide to dilute the maple syrup so that it will take a lot of work to get it that sweet again and it will only run once per year. This is not a retaliatory gesture, nor an act of revenge, but a change made to get the people back on a good course. This is a constant theme in stories in which revenge could occur and doesn't.

Clinical Story

Next, I think about the application of Olivier's ideas to my clinical work. I do work with people who are traumatized – from historical trauma, intergenerational trauma, and ongoing trauma. They are wounded. We start by validating the anger – that these acts should have never happened and that it isn't the person's fault. Often the perpetrators of the violence are long gone or are different people (sobered, former alcoholic, for example) from when the violence occurred. The first order of forgiveness is self-forgiveness. People blame themselves for acts that they could not have committed to themselves.

I think of a woman who was beaten to near death by her older brother and her father and some other men. They were drunk and had decided she had dishonored the family and was a whore (she wasn't). They beat her unconscious and left her to die. By chance (or through spirit intervention), she was found by an early morning hunter. He called the ambulance, and she went to the intensive care unit, where she stayed for several days. When she awoke, she refused to say who had beaten her, though she told me, years later. She left immediately and went to live in Hartford, Connecticut. She returned for the funeral when her older brother overdosed. Her father was no longer drinking, but he was fragile as was her mother. She decided to move home and take care of them. Naturally, this generated conflicting feelings which we had to discuss. She remained angry, even enraged at times, at her father, her older brother, and the other men, most of whom were also dead. Had she forgiven her father in a way, by coming home to help him and her mother? Had she forgiven her brother in a way by coming to his funeral? We worked with her stories about what could have been and what might yet become. We did ceremony. She came to the *inipikaga* that I do. She connected with a cousin and started going to Native American Church meetings. One day, we put all the photographs on chairs, and we duplicated Olivier's process, but without extra people – just their ghosts, captured by the photographs. The result was powerful. As Olivier mentions, the focus is always on our letting go of the toxic energy. We can't change other people; we can only open ourselves to the possibility of change.

Personal Story

I have used Olivier's process to advantage in my own life. I am angry at my father for abandoning me/us. I am angry at my mother for covering up his identity. I am angry at my stepfather for how rejecting he was of me as his only non-biological child. During Olivier's circle of forgiveness in France one day, I made progress in releasing that anger and accepting that these people were scared, almost teenagers, and that my stepfather, as wicked as I perceived him, was tremendously kinder than his parents were to him. I began to appreciate that we are all somewhere on the web that connects us all and that we need to stop judging people because we're not in the same place on the web where they are, and we can't know what forces are affecting them, so how can we criticize anyone. So Olivier's process started my journey toward radical acceptance of these people who made, birthed, and parented me – virtual children themselves at the start of the journey.

Conclusions

With the help of don Miguel Ruiz, Olivier has developed a process that is benefiting people around the globe, one that can produce fantastic results in only two hours' time. Some of that comes from the intentions that people bring to the circle for healing. Some of it comes from the practice of radical acceptance and radical compassion for self and others. However, I suspect one needs to be ready for this process. Those who choose to come, are; those who are not, stay away. Nevertheless, Olivier offers us a fantastic tool for reducing hatred on the planet, for deflecting the urge for revenge, for connecting with each other, and for trying to be the good people that our dogs already think we are.

Preface

I came across forgiveness very unexpectedly in 1999. I had just translated into French, and published, *The Four Agreements* by don Miguel Ruiz (Editions Jouvence). As I told that story in my previous book, *The Gift of Forgiveness*, I had gone to Mexico for two weeks at Teotihuacan to meet the author in person, and attend his teachings.

On the second day, much to my surprise, and thanks to don Miguel, I had a very moving experience of forgiveness though I couldn't have foreseen it in the programme of the workshop. This was to radically change my life. Within a few minutes, the four-step ritual I went through gave me access to the forgiveness I had never thought I would reach, despite my Catholic education, where it plays an essential role. I didn't discover heart-opening on that day in Mexico, but heart *healing*, a means to heal small or deep, rare or numerous wounds that most of us do not fail to accumulate during the better part of our life, especially in childhood.

Though I had already, during twenty years of spiritual life before meeting don Miguel Ruiz, cultivated my inner garden, it took ten more years for the seed he planted to mature, ten years for it to produce a tree whose fruits I could thereafter share. The book, *The Gift of Forgiveness*, in which I related my initiation into forgiveness, and what I had learned from it throughout the years, was first published in English in 2010. It appeared in French eight months later, and has been translated since into eight other languages. My only goal was to share this process with my readers so they would also experience this at home. I had never thought of conducting workshops on forgiveness, and supporting other people on this path.

But two friends, who are both transpersonal psychotherapists, suggested I should set up such workshops to allow those who might want to experience this process to do so in a place where they would feel secure and supported. I took them up on their suggestion but not without some hesitation. Was I entitled to lead others onto this path? Would it work? In going ahead with this project, I had never imagined for one second that this new activity would, within two years, become the most important of the various hats I wear today.

With the unforeseen success I encountered in these workshops, I realized how much we need the means to reach forgiveness. And, to answer those needs, two unexpected turns came from this new awareness.

It started at the end of 2012 when, with my wife Annabelle, we organized the first *Forgiveness Days* in collaboration with the association *Artisans de Paix* (Peacemakers) led by Alain Michel in the Doubs (France) at the well-named *Consolation Val*. The idea underlying this four-day event is that there are no more cure-alls for heart wounds than for those of the body. What suits you at one point in your life is not necessarily adapted for another person, nor is it for yourself at another time of your life.

Hence the importance of having at our disposal a variety of therapies, for healing our heart. So we gathered more than twenty contributors from seven different countries who joined us to offer a wide range of lectures, workshops and ceremonies on how to take the path to forgiveness. This was very much like a great tasting buffet where, with some luck, each participant could find their own way to reach forgiveness at that point in their life. This very first event was so successful, with a total of 200 people attending, that we were prompted to organize a second one at the end of 2014, with as much success.

Faced with the growing number of people wanting to work on forgiveness, I thought we could create *Forgiveness Circles*, following models of healing circles, prayer circles, meditation circles, circles gathering men, or women, and so on. It first occurred to me in Paris, then in Varna (Bulgaria), when within a few months I was invited to lead a two-hour-only workshop to introduce my approach. At first, it seemed impossible to squeeze into two hours what I usually did in two days. But once on location, I was pressed to do what seemed impossible, namely to allow the participants to experience the – well-named – *heart* of the process that would normally take a weekend. And the results went beyond my expectations. In barely two hours, the people attending experienced something that was very much like my own experience in Mexico. Many of them were able to free themselves from the stranglehold around their heart. They were able to feel, sometimes for the first time, a level of love that had been unknown to them until then.

This is why I suggested to people who had already attended a full workshop with me, to follow a training in order to create and lead *Forgiveness Circles* in their town, their area, or their country. Once more, people responded way beyond my wildest expectations. Within only eighteen months, more than forty *Forgiveness Circles* were created in France, Belgium, Switzerland, Polynesia and the West Indies. Over the years that followed, over 250 such Circles were created in 15 different countries (see www.cerclesdepardon.fr).

Since the beginning of this venture, I really feel like I've actually been supporting a process that goes way beyond me. I try to surf on this great and beautiful wave of forgiveness. I try to provide it with adequate channels, where its health-giving waters can freely flow, and touch those who crave drinking it, as others do in different approaches. Each new step naturally follows the previous one.

Today, looking back on all these years gone by since the *Gift of Forgiveness* was published, and since I started leading workshops, I feel the need to share with my readers all the things I have been able to understand and deepen thanks to the rich interactions with the people attending my workshops. This is why I'm writing this book. *Healing the Wounds of the Heart, 15 Obstacles to Forgivenes and How to Overcome Them*, the title of this new book, refers to the most recurrent question I've been asked in lectures and workshops. For many of us, this is the big question about forgiveness. Forgiving the little or big wounds we may have undergone in our childhood, in our relationships, at work or elsewhere. Many people say: "OK, but can Hitler or Bin Laden, a rapist or a paedophile, a murderer or a psychopath be forgiven?"

To give an adequate answer to this question, I thought it was first necessary to redefine what lies behind the word 'forgiving'. Just like many others, the notion of forgiveness has many meanings and very different understandings from one person to another. Throughout the years, I've realized that forgiveness, in our society, is a very vague and imprecise word including a hotchpotch of different things that need to be clearly defined. Before being prepared to forgive anything, we need to know precisely what this approach entails. Have you ever thought about it?

If not, I suggest we start by taking a few minutes to do so.

- Where does your way of seeing forgiveness come from?

- How do you, personally, see it?

- According to you, what are its religious, social, psychological or philosophical tinges?

- Do you find them relevant? Have you questioned them?

- Do you know ways of seeing forgiveness?

In the following pages, we'll start by redefining what forgiveness is, as it will unfold here, on the basis of concrete experiences: first my humble experiences, of course, but especially those of the numerous people who have attended my workshops and *Forgiveness Circles*, and those of the various contributors to the *Forgiveness Days*, and of the witnesses of forgiveness who shared their experience with us.

Then, to better work out what forgiveness really is so we can truly heal the wounds of the heart, we'll approach the many confusions, misunderstandings and simplifications it has undergone, in how many of us see it to begin with, based on what we hear about it, around us. These are the many obstacles to dismiss or overcome on the path to forgiveness. And on top of that, we have unconscious mechanisms, automatic reflexes of the heart and the mind, that make us react to the wounds and violent deeds undergone in a way that may hinder forgiveness rather than encourage it. By revealing them, we'll be able to consciously adopt other attitudes and other ways of being, and be much more successful in implementing forgiveness in our lives.

To not remain only within the field of thought – however important and necessary it is – the fifteen major hindrances to forgiveness that will be developed here will be interspersed with stories and first-hand accounts on the one hand, and with the presentation of various tools for forgiveness on the other hand. Throughout the following pages, you will find:

Great Stories of Forgiveness

Originally published by the *Forgiveness Project* (see page 154), these very moving stories are all genuine ones. You will discover how people like you and me, brutally confronted with the unspeakable, managed to find their path to forgiveness and peace of heart. Their stories are highly inspiring.

Testimonies of Forgiveness

For me it's useful to share some of the many testimonies I have received throughout the years of people who were able to make their way towards forgiveness in the workshops and *Gift of Forgiveness* circles I lead. The examples of others is always a source of inspiration and encouragement for oneself.

Four Approaches to Forgiveness

I've chosen to introduce you to four practical methods of forgiveness that I've had the opportunity to experiment with myself: *Ho'oponopono*, Colin Tipping's *Radical Forgiveness*, the *Nine Steps to Forgive For Good* by Dr Fred Luskin, and the *Gift of Forgiveness* I received from don Miguel Ruiz.

Redefining forgiveness as it is suggested here, and pointing out the obstacles to overcome along the way, along with these first-hand testimonies, should shed new light on the main question always asked about forgiveness – *Can everything be forgiven?* – and should therefore lead to a much richer and more relevant answer than a mere "yes" or "no". As Jewish wisdom has it, "With two solutions to choose from, let's choose the third!"

From the bottom of my heart,
I wish you a gentle path towards forgiveness.

Olivier Clerc, November 2021

PS. As a bonus, I have added to this book the *Metaphor of the Two Clouds* that I use in my workshops, as a transpersonal and inspired way of perceiving and understanding violence, love and forgiveness (see page 137).

Part 1

Forgiveness Defined

Forgiveness—
What Is It Really?

⁓⁓⁓⁓⁓⁓

J ust like other notions, forgiveness has very different meanings
for each one of us. For example, what do you think of first when
you hear this word?

For some, it recalls being obliged to "say sorry" either at home or
at school, for having treated someone else badly. We often experienced forgiveness as humiliating because it was forced upon us with
authority, so it was seldom genuine. There must be good intentions
underlying this educational reflex, or they do not really reach their
goal, and those who have suffered from it may have been marked by
a very basic – to say the least – understanding of forgiveness.

For others, forgiveness plays an important part, especially in
the Christian tradition I was raised in. It evokes reciting the Our
Father prayer (*"forgive us our trespasses as we forgive those who trespass
against us"*) or the practice of confession, with the hope of being
forgiven for our sins, real ones . . . or ones invented for the occasion.
These practices, whether performed mechanically or as the result of
a deliberate and thoroughly reflected approach, may imprint us all
in very different ways. Some of us may remember something artificial and somewhat useless, while for others it may have become a
genuine and beneficial spiritual practice.

As far as I am concerned, I had to wait until I was almost forty
for this founding experience in Mexico, referred to in the preface, to
start a deep reflection on what forgiveness really meant for me. And
I added to that a regular practice of the ritual I had received.

In fact, I had never really much wondered about what forgiving
or asking for forgiveness actually meant. Theoretically, it was obvious. You make a mistake, or you misbehave towards someone? Then
you ask for their forgiveness. Conversely: you have yourself been
the victim of the misdeeds of someone? You do your best to forgive
them. OK.

And how does this work?

In practice, it turns out to be much more complicated in both cases. Even when you acknowledge having done wrong, it's not easy to ask for forgiveness: you either feel like you are giving the other some power over you, or as if you were vulnerable or even in danger. And when you're the one who has suffered, granting forgiveness may turn out to be very difficult despite all your great intentions, even if you consider it to be the right thing to do, or that you *should* do it.

Why? Why is forgiveness, often a very complicated thing for most of us, especially as we are reminded of it every day in the news of the world?

It's maybe, precisely, because we do not have a clear idea of what forgiveness really means. Having a vague and approximate understanding of it may result in implementing the practice of forgiveness in a hazardous or tedious way. In fact, we do not really understand how it expresses itself within us. So, it remains relatively mysterious, and does not seem to depend on our will. That's undoubtedly the reason why many believers are convinced that forgiveness depends on *His* will, that it falls within the sole province of divine mercy. It is, admittedly, a respectable option, though difficult to understand, and especially difficult to implement for non-believers.

In the *Forgiveness Circles* that are held once a month in many cities, forgiveness is first and foremost something that is *experienced*. The mind is temporarily bypassed. In many cases, people come with loads of questions, even with mental blocks, doubting they will ever find the forgiveness they long for. It's not intellectually that they find their answers in these circles, but through a personal first-hand experience. That will then lead to a new understanding of what forgiveness is, thereafter based on their personal experience.

But as this is to be in book form, and not within a circle of people, I'll first try to draft a new vision of forgiveness, hoping it will enable you to practice alone or within a group, with the help of various means at your disposal, some of which are introduced throughout these pages.

There are three different metaphors that are dear to me, and that highlight this new way of seeing forgiveness, each one shedding a new and complementary light onto it.

Forgiveness or Healing
the Wounds of the Heart

I magine you've cut your leg. You bleed a little. If you don't do any-thing and you just wait, the wound may eventually get infected. We all know that, so our reflex is to disinfect the wound as soon as possible, and then let the body cure on its own. If we're more seri-ously wounded, we may need a doctor for stitches, before our body, once more, undertakes its own healing process.

But now, what about the wounds of our heart, or our feelings instead of those of the body?

As you must have experienced it yourself, most of us – maybe all of us – reach adulthood having suffered and accumulated all kinds of emotional wounds, small ones or deep ones, occasionally or frequently. We have practically all been wounded in childhood, adolescence or adulthood. Our heart has suffered blows. Some of us even say our heart was "broken" more than once.

What has happened to these wounds?

Many of them have never healed. Admittedly, the small ones have healed themselves. But not the deeper ones, the more seri-ous ones. Those have usually remained open, or become emotional cysts, ready to reopen, and to exude again all kinds of toxic and negative emotions. Were we able to see our "emotional body" – as we sometimes call the seat of our feelings and emotions – we'd probably see it covered with wounds of all sizes, from head to foot, more or less infected or scarred. It all depends. It's our common lot, except in rare cases.

As for curing the physical body, whether we support allopathy or not, we must admit that modern surgery works wonders. It man-ages to stitch up accidentally amputated parts of the body, to restore the integrity of people who were left in pieces after a fall in the mountains or a car accident, or other similar feats.

But what medicine do we have to heal our heart's wounds and allow them to form scars? Apparently, we are lagging way behind in this field, seeing the state in which so many of us are, sometimes for many years.

Yet this medicine, or rather these medicines, really exist too. Forgiveness is precisely their keystone. Forgiveness – as we will see it here – is indeed the healing, the curing of the heart's wounds. It's the balm that can cure them. It's the remedy to be applied to emotional poisons such as hatred, rancour and resentment. Without forgiveness, healing cannot be achieved. The wound has only been clumsily hidden. We hide it behind the stories we tell ourselves, so it's bound to reopen, and bleed again, at any time.

> "Forgiveness – as we will consider it here – is indeed the healing, the curing of the heart's wounds. It's the balm that can cure them. It's the remedy to be applied to emotional poisons such as hatred, rancour and resentment."

This definition in itself radically changes our way of understanding and considering forgiveness. Implementing forgiveness, bearing this new perspective in mind, means healing *my* wounds, taking care of *my* heart, and freeing *myself* from the stranglehold of hatred, and the desire for revenge. It's first and foremost a gift to myself. For, if I can't forgive, I'm the one who really suffers. I'm the one who keeps my wounds open and purulent. I'm the one intoxicating myself with my own negative emotional secretions: rancour, resentment, repressed angers, silent rages and so on. Only forgiveness can bring me the healing I long for. That's what can put an end to my sufferings, and allow my heart to love again.

This parallel drawn between physical and emotional wounds, between what affects the integrity of our body or our heart, has a lot to teach us if we take the trouble to go deeper into the matter. For instance, it was not so long ago when we could only resort to prayers when faced with illnesses that we can easily cure today. We used to be completely helpless confronted with these diseases. Nothing could be done to fight them, so there was no other option than to leave it up to God, to something bigger than us, . . . or to surrender to despair.[1] Since those days, medicine has made

---

[1] In saying this, I do not underestimate the value of prayer.

continuous progress. Year after year, more and more diseases are cured. And we are each, individually, able to take care of our own health and to heal many benign illnesses. Curing methods and treatments were discovered by people who then taught them to others, to be spread wherever they were deemed useful.

Likewise, for a long time, healing the heart's wounds has seemed to depend on divine intervention or on blessings from above. Even when we wanted to forgive, and longed for healing, our heart would no more obey our will than our physical body would obey its healing process. For a number of years however, "heart medicine", emotional medicine, has also made a lot of progress. Psychotherapy, in particular, has been enriched by various approaches that enable us to take the path towards healing the heart's wounds. Forgiveness is not always included in that process because some believe – wrongly – that it's a religious concern, while others bluntly consider it belongs to the past; it is obsolete. Yet forgiveness is coming back and taking its rightful essential place. It's like the ultimate crowning achievement of this healing process, thanks to our gradual understanding of it, as we are doing it here. New tools, new ways of approaching forgiveness – including many non-religious ones – have appeared and are beginning to spread here and there, wherever people need them. Several are introduced within these pages. Some of them need to be approached in groups, or in circles, while others may be used individually. For some people, these practices become a true *heart hygiene*. And this leads us to our second metaphor, after the following first testimony.

The Forgiveness Project
The Story of Mary Foley (England)

*I knew that if I didn't forgive,
anger and bitterness would turn me into a person
Charlotte would not have liked.*

In 2005 Mary Foley's 15-year-old daughter, Charlotte, was murdered during a birthday party in East London. In February 2006, 18-year-old Beatriz Martins-Paes was jailed for life for the unprovoked attack.

"It was in the early hours of Sunday morning that the police rang to tell me Charlotte had been stabbed. It was like being catapulted into a different world, but still death was the last thing on my mind. Even at the hospital, when I saw all these young people distraught and sobbing, it still didn't sink in. It was only when three doctors came into the room that I knew something terrible had happened. 'I'm so sorry, Mrs. Foley,' one said, 'but we couldn't save her.'

"I didn't know what to do. I immediately went hot. I walked up and down the corridor of the hospital. I couldn't believe it. For the days that followed I couldn't function. People came to the house but I felt paralyzed. I wasn't sure any of it was real.

"Finally, after two weeks, it sunk in that Charlotte didn't just die; she had been murdered. Murdered by Beatriz Martins-Paes. But then I began hearing rumors that it was another girl's fault – a girl who was supposed to have been at the party but never turned up. This girl had an ongoing feud with Beatriz and had made arrangements to have it out with her at the party. So Beatriz had come armed with two knives; all hyped up, smoking weed and ready to do damage. Unfortunately it was Charlotte who felt Beatriz's wrath.

"For the first few days I didn't think about forgiveness. I just thought about my baby, Charlotte, not knowing she was going to be stabbed that night, and me not being there to hold her in my arms. It was very hard to swallow. I had so much hope for Charlotte. She was growing up into a beautiful young lady who wanted to be a social worker and work with young people. All her future promise had been snatched away in an instant.

"Two weeks after Charlotte's death – during which time I prayed and held onto my faith, receiving comfort and support from Christ and from my husband – God gave me the strength and grace to forgive. I didn't say anything to my family at that time because I felt they may not have understood. When I eventually told my husband, he said, 'I'm going to get there too one day.' But for myself I knew that if I didn't forgive, anger and bitterness would turn me into a person Charlotte would not have liked: A person that none of my family or friends would have liked, for that matter.

"At first forgiveness was about freeing me, because without forgiveness I felt I would have ended up a prisoner. I didn't think much about the perpetrator. It was only in court, when I heard about the physical domestic abuse Beatriz's mother encountered, and about Beatriz herself being exposed to that violence, that I started to feel some compassion for her and to understand why she might have done what she did. But there is still no excuse for her: she had a choice and she alone made that choice.

"Forgiveness relieved me of a burden I didn't want to carry. It has allowed me to use what had happened to Charlotte to educate young people about the consequences of carrying a knife for protection.

"Some months after the trial, Beatriz wrote to me saying she was very sorry and that she didn't mean to kill Charlotte. She said it had been a moment of madness. I was pleased to receive the letter and wrote back telling her I'd forgiven her. Later she sent a 14-page letter with more detail about her life and asking me about Charlotte. I was struck that both these girls had shared similar concerns and insecurities. So I wrote back again, this time telling her all about my beautiful daughter.

"It was nearly a year before the next letter came, and this one was different. In it Beatriz said that I was the only person who could help her. It was a real cry for help – a desperate letter. She's obviously carrying so much pain and guilt. I now feel ready to meet Beatriz. It would help me and I also think it would help her find closure. She'll be in her thirties when she finally gets out and I'd love her to have a great career and a positive mindset. Most of all I'd love her to value her life and the lives of others.

"Some people tell me I'm brave and strong, but others don't say much. Although no one has come up to me and said, "you can't have loved your daughter to forgive her killer", I'm sure that's what they think at times. And I understand that, because some people are disgusted by the very idea of forgiveness. It can seem like an act of betrayal. But, on the contrary, I think it's an act of freedom."

Forgiveness or Showering the Heart

Now let's come to our second metaphor. We all know that one of the factors that has contributed most to the decline of diseases in the last centuries is merely the development of hygiene. Today still, the well-known gastroenteritis epidemics – that occur almost every year in France – are mainly due to insufficient hygiene.

However, considerable progress has been made in this field in the last century. To support this, one evening, I switched on my television and unexpectedly watched a programme on palaces (I believe it was *Des Racines et des Ailes*). Many of these magnificent hotels, built in the 19th or in the early 20th century in exceptional surroundings, catering for very well-to-do clients, showed – at the time of their construction – a distinctive feature that struck me. It so happens that they only had a single bathroom . . . per floor! Yes, what you're reading is right, *a single bathroom per floor* and not per room. Why? It was the state of physical hygiene in those days:

an occasional bath was more than enough, and showers were still unknown. By contrast today, even the cheapest hotel includes at least a basic shower in each room. Nowadays, everybody finds it normal to wash every day: nobody feels like annoying others with their body odours, faintly concealed by perfumes, like in the past.

By comparison, what about emotional hygiene this time?

Because we've not been educated in that field, most of us have a heart that is burdened with old, foul emotions or – here comes another image – we have accumulated important layers of *emotional cholesterol* that line our arteries, and block the free and fluid flow of our full love. Of course, we've learned how to put up a front or a good show, how to hide under an attitude that is the result of all our painful emotions. We do not really know how to get rid of them, but we *perspire* them anyway, as we can clearly see in other people.

Forgiveness is precisely the shower of the heart. Very simple methods like the *Gift of Forgiveness* (see p. 117) or *Ho'oponopono* (see p. 98), when practiced regularly in the evening before going to sleep, can literally wash the unpleasant emotions accumulated during the day in our heart. And it can avoid their progressive accumulation and crystallization within us. Those who make a habit of doing it will eventually notice that even the quality of their dreams is transformed. Instead of using the REM sleep as a nightly garbage collector, in charge of doing its best to evacuate the emotional waste built up during the day, an emotional "cleansing" consciously made just before sleeping, helps us to go to sleep lightheartedly, relieving us of useless burdens. The soul of the sleeper can then rise up to brighter realms, and return in the morning having experienced dreams of a somewhat better quality.

"Forgiveness is the shower of the heart. It can literally wash the unpleasant emotions accumulated during the day from our heart, and in this way avoid their progressive accumulation and crystallization within us."

There is another advantage to this emotional hygiene, this shower of the heart. It's a kind of everyday training, thanks to which I gradually increase my ability to deal with the difficult or painful emotions that may appear in my life. If I do my best everyday to wash my heart of the little emotional sediments that may reduce the natural flow of love, I then acquire a know-how that may, should it happen, help me face much more difficult hardships. The heart (or the emotional body) can be trained just like the physical body. It can also become more resistant, more flexible, more powerful.

Incidentally, an ideal education should devote as much time to our mental, emotional and physical faculties instead of exclusively focusing on developing the intellect, leaving the body with only a few hours of physical education, and completely neglecting the heart. We would then avoid raising children with an overly developed mental state who, on the one hand, have no idea about healthy food and the preservation of a healthy body, and on the other hand do not know how to interact harmoniously with themselves and with others. A real educational project today should aim at fighting emotional, relational and sanitary illiteracy that wreaks havoc throughout life, on an individual level, as well as on a collective level.

Until this pedagogical dream comes true, learning how to shower our heart ourselves, how to let the water of forgiveness wash us from everything that could clog it up, and also teaching our children how to do it like brushing their teeth, means taking up an emotional hygiene which is the best of preventions against the gradual loss of our full capacity to love.

Some of you may attend fitness centres for weekly cardio trainings: you stimulate your heart physically to keep it fit throughout the years. It's a healthy habit, that could be happily coupled with an equivalent for the emotional heart, because of the emotional wounds life sometimes has in store for us.

The metaphor of forgiveness seen as a shower of the heart brings another interesting component as we redefine forgiveness here: that of repetition, of consistency. Imagine someone saying "OK! I've had my shower for this year!" You might possibly think, "This is a strange way of seeing physical cleanliness!" Well it's the same thing for the shower of the heart.

A single shower, though powerful and beneficial it may be, is not enough, even if some think so at the end of a session of *Forgiveness*

Circle or *Ho'oponopono*. Because every week, if not every day, brings its share of dust or emotional "dirt" during our interactions with others, unless we live alone, cut off from the world (and even then).

The emotional hyper-activity of many people, in particular in big cities, where anything can set off a fit of bad temper – the hoot of a horn or a disproportionate remark – is the symptom of a lengthy accumulation of negative emotions, angers, frustrations, humiliations. And a mere trifle is sometimes enough to rekindle them like embers. A regular practice of forgiveness can help you first drain off this emotional overflow, then avoid a new accumulation through a simple, everyday hygiene of the heart.

Véronique's Testimony

"I took part in a *Gift of Forgiveness* workshop in Toulouse (France). As I expressed it at the end: wow! For me it was a revelation. I became aware of my misconceived beliefs on forgiveness. I used to think I would only be able to forgive the people who had abused me when they acknowledged their deed. I became aware of the fact that this belief was fuelling my wounds.

"I was able to make the difference between forgiving and condoning. This workshop allowed me to bring this awareness into the heart instead of the mind.

"I also realized that I did not forgive myself much of anything, that the one I *had* to forgive first and foremost was myself. I was able to see and feel our resistance to receiving, the resistance of the ego that cherishes and feeds on our position of victim.

"What remains of this workshop is the shower of light that has since become a regular, energizing, and purifying practice."

Forgiveness: A Revival of Love

I really like this third metaphor when speaking about forgiveness: the revival of love. It sometimes happens that, after a tragic event – be it betrayal, bereavement, a violent break-up, or even ill-treatment – something within us fades and dies. We feel so wounded and so bruised that an inner voice cries "Never again!" Our inner source shuts down, is drained and dries up. I will never love again. I never want to love again. It's too painful. So our heart dries up. Our inner garden becomes a desert. Life loses its flavour, we no longer have any taste for life. Most great stories of forgiveness mention this time spent in the wilderness. Worse than the desert, it's sometimes a real inner ice field: hatred has turned everything into ice, everything has been frozen and mortified. A real icy desert.

So, whenever people manage to implement forgiveness in their lives, what we witness really looks like a rebirth, a revival of love that was once dead. They come back to life, their heart learns how to love again: their love, once dead, is born again.

We can point out too that a love that has experienced the darkness of the soul, some time in the wilderness, has a unique quality, and is very different from before. It has stood the test. It is reborn, it has risen from its ashes just like a phoenix. "Love is greater than death": this is what forgiveness is all about, in its highest and most difficult aspect.

> "Whenever people manage to implement forgiveness in their lives, what we witness really looks like a rebirth, a revival of love that was once dead. They come back to life, their heart learns how to love again: their love once dead is born again."

If we consider this symbolically, it really is what life, death and the Resurrection of Christ teach us, as it's told in the Gospels: love prevails over death. Far from historical or theological debates over the life of Jesus, the impact his life has had on all five continents for the past two millenniums is, in itself, an illustration of the reality and the power of this message of love and forgiveness, whether we are Christians or not.

To those of you who may still be in the darkness, in the wilderness of their heart, to those of you who might believe love is forever dead in your life, with this third metaphor you may catch a glimpse of the possibility of rebirth. The dried-up spring can flow again. The desert can blossom again. The ice can melt.

Here again, the stories gathered throughout the years by the *Forgiveness Project* show that people from all walks of life, of all ages and all denominations, have managed to experience such a revival of the heart thanks to the alchemy of forgiveness. These are not historical characters, nor are they prophets of former times. These are people like you and me, ordinary people who have undergone something terribly out of the ordinary and who, in one way or another, have been able to implement forgiveness. One of them, whose 16-year-old daughter was murdered at a party by a girl her age, tells us in fact that when she had reached the point of forgiving her, the emotion she felt was of the same nature and intensity . . . as when she gave birth to her own daughter! Can there be a more beautiful illustration of a rebirth brought by forgiveness?

Mylène's Testimony

"Since many of us were holding a grudge against Life, when the idea of asking Life for forgiveness was brought up in the *Gift of Forgiveness* workshop, I was shattered: yes, I still held it against Life since it had taken a beloved husband from one of my friends!

"I was saying 'Yes' to Life, but it was a 'Yes, but'. I was using what trials Life had dealt her to refuse to love: why should we love if Life takes our beloved away from us? Why should we have a strong inner bond with a man who would either not feel the same love (owing to a yet ill-digested break-up), or who would die? I didn't want to love anymore!

"It just so happens that this particular friend of mine was attending that workshop. And later on, she was the first person

I asked for forgiveness! I asked her, within myself, to forgive me for having used her bereavement to nourish my anger towards Life . . .

"I cried a lot during that workshop, because the first words triggered my awareness, and I realized how imprisoned I was inside by this persistent grudge, how detrimental it had been to me, and to me alone (fatigue, depression, etc.).

"About two months ago, I felt my heart reopen again: it had been progressive throughout the year, but then I felt real joy, real happiness when faced with one of my daughters' happiness. For months and even years, I had been intellectually glad but not happy within my heart. I had not been able to be really delighted over my children's happiness. It has come back, and I feel very grateful."

Judgement and Forgiveness

The other interesting avenue worth exploring to better understand and redefine forgiveness is to examine the link between forgiveness and judgement. It's what I remember of my religious education that prompted my reflection on this subject. In my workshops, I actually tell about being raised in the Catholic denomination: I was baptized, went to church every Sunday until I was sixteen, made my first communion and then the solemn one, confirmation. Being gifted with a very good memory, I can still recite by heart – thirty-seven years later! – whole pieces of Catholic liturgy, and many extracts from the Old and the New Testaments. But it was only twenty or thirty years later that I realized I had not understood many of these writings, despite hearing all those sermons. I felt I had missed a lot of the deep meaning of some of those sentences. Is there anyone in particular who has never read or heard these very renowned words of Jesus on his cross?: "Father forgive them, for they don't know what they're doing." (Luke 23:4) I, for one, had heard that dozens and dozens of times, at least. But it was only after my first experience with forgiveness in Mexico that I was suddenly struck by how obvious it was while re-reading this quotation.

Though Jesus is, for a Christian, the second figure of the Trinity, he does not put himself into the position of forgiving. He does not say: "I forgive you, you don't know what you are doing." But, as the son of God, couldn't he do it? Well, no. He appeals to higher than himself. "*Father*, forgive them . . ." Why? The answer may be found in another of his sayings: "I don't judge anyone." (John, 8:15) If Jesus judges no-one, he has no-one to forgive either. He leaves judgement and forgiveness to higher than himself.

To my mind, this underlines the close link there is between judgement and forgiveness. And we don't have a clear idea of that. If I feel entitled to forgive, it's also because I believe I am allowed to judge. The word judgement here is to be understood as I define it in *J'arrête de (me) juger,*[2] which is a three-level standpoint from which observing a blameworthy act (i.e., an unbiased fact) is doubled by negative emotions (like hatred or fury), and is backed by the building of a scenario, mental projections, and various assumptions (or biased interpretations). If I feel I can grant forgiveness to someone, it's because I have first used my judgement as it's defined above. I did not merely content myself with noticing what acts that person committed, I also "condemned" that person within me, which means that I rejected, excluded and hated him or her. In the most severe cases, I might also have wished for their death, or for their worst sufferings.

So, the forgiveness I believe I can grant others, if I really look into myself, isn't it rather the word I use for *my* own hatred, for giving up the accusations I made that pinned *me* down, just like a three-ton burden I had undertaken?

"There is a close link between judgement and forgiveness.
. . . If I feel entitled to forgive, it is also because I believe
I am also allowed to judge."

---

[2] Olivier Clerc, *J'arrête de (me) juger* (Eyrolles, 2014). The title means translated: "I will stop judging myself."

I need to warn you right now, and we'll come back to this later when we deal with the obstacles to forgiveness: giving up the act of judging is not lacking discernment. It's not becoming stupid, accepting everything, condoning everything, or excusing everything. It only means that you stop hating. We can objectively see the wrongs done to us, we can also allow ourselves all the needed space to express our sorrow, our pain, our suffering . . . without necessarily letting the mechanism of revenge or the desire to suffer settle in, and without allowing our heart to secrete lethal poisons like resentment, rancour, and plain hatred *within ourself*.

There is a certain amount of letting go in forgiveness, when letting go first means giving up the judgements that destroy *us* and the fury that consumes *us* when it comes with challenging the superiority of our position, from which we feel entitled to judge others without appeal, and sentence them to execution. After judgement comes humility, whose root refers to *humus*, the earth, and to becoming *human*: I step down from the ivory tower of my inner judge, I dump my load of accusations onto the ground, and I leave fair judgement and forgiveness to higher than me, to the Skies and to the Earth. By *dumping my load*, I can – literally and figuratively – find the way to discharge the millions of volts of hatred that were threatening to destroy *me*.

Going from judgement to forgiveness is a surprising reversal of position. The ritual I was given by Miguel Ruiz consists first in encouraging this reversal of position by *asking for forgiveness*, though paradoxical it may seem, to someone who has suffered, and who instead would rather expect to be entitled to receive a request for forgiveness.

The key to this paradox (see p.116), is that we don't ask for forgiveness for what the other has done to us, of course, because that person is the only one to bear responsibility for the act. We ask for forgiveness for our own hatred, for the way we might have used, for too long, the deeds of another to fuel our resentment, and as a consequence to keep our own wounds from healing. In fact, we ask for forgiveness to free ourselves. To no longer give others the power to decide how we feel inside. To recover our own power, and our share of responsibility. Thus this other paradox: forgiveness is a virtue that seems to disappear when we exercise it. In asking for forgiveness inside, in relinquishing my judgements, in ceasing to hate . . . it's the very need to *forgive* that seems to disappear with it! Who am I to judge? Therefore, who am I to forgive?

Without judging anyone in saying this – because this is just where we stand today in our society – through lack of knowledge, and lack of education, we often become our own torturer without knowing it. In the wake of the harm we actually suffered, our unconscious and uninformed heart and mind lock us up within an inner nightmarish cocoon, the web of our thoughts and feelings – stemming from actual deeds – that end up magnifying, worsening and making them endure.

By working consciously on non-judgement and forgiveness, we manage to become aware of this mechanism, to see how we function emotionally and intellectually, then to change tack, to stop this vicious weaving of threads in order to recover inner freedom and light. We're not compelled to remain in the cold darkness of our cocoon of hatred, passively waiting for a miracle to tear it open, and give us access again to bright daylight and the warm sun. We can act ourselves, from within. We can consciously stop what we were doing unknowingly until then. And as soon as it stops being fed by our own thoughts and feelings, the cocoon cracks, softens up, and ends up falling into pieces. Reaching forgiveness, from this perspective, is bringing the process of judgement, whose ceaseless weaving has cut us from light and love, to an end.

> "We are not compelled to remain in our cocoon, in the cold darkness of our hatred, passively waiting for a miracle to tear it open and give us access again to bright daylight and the warm sun. We can act ourselves, from within."

Taking into account the link between judgement and forgiveness sheds new light and broadens our knowledge of forgiveness in yet other ways, as you might have noticed. Here, it's more a matter of doing than undoing. There is no outer salvation to expect, we can apply ourselves to dismantling the bars of the prison we unknowingly built ourselves.

The inability to forgive, to which so many of us have been confronted at one point or another, takes on new light. It's a fact that I cannot forgive if all of my energy is focused on judging, detesting, hating, being full of morbid intentions. It would be like trying to speed up when my other foot is on the brake. It would be like trying to heal a wound while constantly cultivating it, displaying it every day for everybody to see, spreading it open to show how deep it is and the damage done. Release the brake! Leave your wounds alone, and your body will heal them itself. Stop judging, stop exuding the pus of hatred and your wounds will heal themselves. There are methods for that, tools you can use. No need to reinvent. No need either to sit in a corner moping, nor to wait for mercy to come to you some day.

It's basically our ignorance and our unconsciousness of the way we function – for example imitating the examples of others when we were very young – that drive us into painful situations, with these wounds of the heart that make us suffer so. And we have no idea how to pull ourselves out of these situations since we are not clearly aware of how we got into them in the first place. The good news is that we can learn to forgive. Yes, let's say it again: *we can learn to forgive*. We can gain the knowledge and awareness needed to undo what we did inadvertently. We can re-educate our mind and our heart so that, from the unconscious enemies they too often are, they may become truly conscious allies. No-one says it's easy, nor that it can be done in one day, but it's possible. And knowing it's possible, that there is hope, is a lot already for whoever thought they would be doomed to spend the rest of their life in misery, with a dried up heart and unable to love again.

Dominique's Testimony

"The *Forgiveness Circle* in itself is an extraordinary moment. Facing each person, looking them straight in the eyes and asking them for forgiveness though we don't even know them? What a strong inner effect! It was strange to experience how some people caused so much emotion within me. And experiencing how this request for forgiveness can take on different colours, depending on the person in front of me, was very strange. Very strange indeed!

"When I came back from that weekend, I wanted to re-experience being in front of each person to become aware of whom or what I was asking for forgiveness from. I wanted to understand what each person had awakened in me when I was asking for forgiveness. I expected to recall some people in particular, whom I wanted to ask for forgiveness. But that's not at all what happened. In doing this, I realized that each person played the part of a mirror to myself. Each person sent a different aspect back to me, subtle aspects of my very own self. I then became aware of how much I judge myself! That was a revelation.

"I then felt compelled to accept, little by little, these different aspects of myself and to stop judging myself so harshly. It's time for me to take the trouble of loving myself, of accepting all of my multi-faceted self, despite its various shades, and to stop judging myself . . .

"Since then, I've been especially marked by the notion of acceptance, and by not trying to be perfect anymore (what is being perfect anyway? We are all, basically, perfect!). This issue was raised during the weekend, but it has become strikingly evident since, thanks to what I experienced.

"In fact, I have the feeling that I'm on the way to becoming much more aware of things, that this process is quicker than before, and that the Forgiveness Workshop is one of the great steps that encouraged this process."

Forgiving and Asking for Forgiveness

When I had to declare my book *The Gift of Forgiveness* to the Swiss association of writers, I discovered, to my great surprise, that there was another work bearing the same name: a five-act play, that had neither been published nor performed to that day, by someone called Bertrand Hourcade, a Frenchman living in Switzerland. So I approached him, and we warmly exchanged our respective books. His play taught me many things. It stages Pope John Paul II, and the people surrounding him at the Vatican at the time when he was the victim of a murder attempt by a young Turk that almost killed him. As soon as he regained consciousness, the Pope immediately granted forgiveness to his quasi-murderer, and they corresponded for some time. In the years following that event, as I discovered thanks to this play, John Paul II would be the Pope who would most *ask for forgiveness* in the name of the institution he represented, the Catholic church. I was only aware of one or two of them, those that were most publicized (in particular concerning the Jews or the Inquisition), but the list is impressive.

John Paul II's life is a wide-scale illustration of what we too can verify: the very close link there is between *forgiving* and *asking for forgiveness*. To be honest, the link is so tight that we may as well consider these two verbs as two sides of the same coin, or as two opposite doors giving access to the same sacred space of forgiveness.

What conclusion can we draw from this observation?

If you cannot open the door to *forgiving*, if it remains closed, despite your efforts and knocking on it, because your heart refuses it, because something within you resists and prevents you from doing it, you may perhaps reach the same space when going through the opposite door, the one *asking for forgiveness*.

How is that?

When I find it impossible to "for-*give*", something within me *holds* a grudge. My mind blocks my heart. It dries it up, cools it, and hardens it. When this occurs, I feel at best a lack of concern, a lack of feelings and emotions. My life takes on a desert-like aspect in which nothing has any interest, taste or flavour. At worse, my heart distills hatred and wants to return evil for evil. In this state, I feel severed from love, from life, from the others. My heart is one:

a single hateful relationship is enough to contaminate all others, including the people that are dearest to me.

> "If you cannot open the door to *forgiving*, if it remains closed despite your efforts and your knocking on it because your heart refuses it, because something within you resists and prevents you from doing it, you may perhaps reach the same space when going through the opposite door, the one *asking for forgiveness*."

The unexpected way out from what seems like a dead-end, is to ask myself for forgiveness. Why? And to whom or to what? . . . I can ask Love with a capital L to forgive me, for having cut myself off from it, from this source that gives life to all beings and all things, including myself. If I feel up to it, I can also ask for forgiveness from whoever did me wrong, not for what that person did to me – the only one to blame – but for the way I identified with these negative acts, the way that person was reduced to a shadow, and the way I used that person to cultivate *my own* negative feelings.

Learning to *ask for forgiveness* is a practice that can be found in Judaism for example, but also in the *Ho'oponopono* method, as well as in the *Gift of Forgiveness* that I teach. Its surprising effect is that it suddenly makes a breach in ourselves because it changes our viewpoint and our efforts. I don't look down anymore, from the top of my judgements, at the one who hurt me. I look up now, at Love, at Life, at the divine for those who are believers, with all humility: I let go, I give up again to this energy I have cut myself off from, the lack of which affects me first. As a result, contact is re-established, I feel reconnected to something bigger than myself, with the energy of love flowing through me again.

This paradoxical reversal of position – that we have to experience ourselves to measure its power and simplicity – frees us from something that is stuck within us and bypasses our mental obstacles to forgiveness, in a way that can even amaze us.

When I *held* a grudge, I felt knotted, stuck, locked up, nothing could flow any more within me, and I was denying myself my own vital flow. As soon as I open up to this *gift*, to this *forgiveness*, life and love start flowing again, everything comes alive again. And when I express my wish for forgiveness from above, the opening it creates up there allows the door at the bottom to open up to the people I couldn't forgive before. In opening my heart on one side, it opens the door on the other side too: this metaphor is all the more meaningful as the physical heart can no longer give – in other words it cannot send blood to the whole body – when it cannot receive it from the other side. Likewise, if the heart cannot give, it cannot receive any more. When it cuts itself off from receiving, it has nothing to give any more.

It's the same thing for love, and also for forgiveness which is love reborn. If I block my love, I also don't receive any love. If I cannot grant forgiveness, I also deny myself the one I might be granted. In a time when *channeling* is trendy, we sometimes forget the very simple truth that we are all channels, we don't *produce* love, we let it – or not – flow through us, giving ourselves life, before doing good to others. We are receivers and transmitters. Knowing that, you can work both ways and, if it's stuck on one side, try the other. Love to be loved. Ask for forgiveness to manage to grant forgiveness. Or, as Daniel Pennac[3] used to do with the dunces he took care of, teach others to end up understanding yourself. To re-establish communication, or circulation both ways.

---

[3] Daniel Pennac, *Chagrin d'école* (Gallimard, 2007).

Thomas's Testimony

"My first experience of the *Gift of Forgiveness* occurred after Olivier Clerc had delivered a lecture at the *Café de l'Amour* (Love Café) in Paris. At the time, I was in conflict with a person in my professional life. I still felt some bitterness and resentment towards him although I longed to let go and turn the page. This was the context I was in when I attended the lecture, and Olivier suggested I could go beyond forgiving the one who had offended me, to ask him for forgiveness myself.

"My first reaction was to reject the idea: 'It's the other one who messed around and hurt me in the first place and I should be the one to ask forgiveness?! . . . That's going too far! And what next? Thank him? . . .' Yes, as we will see later.

"However, I welcomed the suggestion of asking for forgiveness, and let it brew, contemplating it. And I slowly started to practice. Just to see . . . Every time the shape of the person appeared to me as an emotional burden, I would ask for forgiveness. And something clicked.

"When I asked this shape for forgiveness, the war I was waging against it stopped. I stopped projecting negative feelings onto it, and so stopped fueling them within me. On the contrary in fact, I would even restore this shape within me. Or, should I say, I restored my projection on this shape, as if there had been two superimposed shapes:

- The real person, the one concerned.
- And above that person, my projection on that person.

"In asking for forgiveness, I was restoring my projection. It's quite subtle and difficult to explain in words. I can only suggest you each try it and make your own experience. As for me, I realized that by asking this shape for forgiveness, I was asking for forgiveness for all the hatred, anger and negativity I was projecting onto it. And I was the first victim of that process by exuding it within me.

"I kept on asking the shape for forgiveness, and this is how the burden I was projecting onto it quickly dissolved. I reintegrated the shape in my heart, as pure energy."

Forgiveness and Humility

As a final point, let us add here that there is no forgiveness without humility. The forgiveness that we pour onto others, that we grant them with magnanimity (or even condescension), is not genuine forgiveness. It's arrogance in disguise. It comes from the mind and not from the heart. The emotional wound is not healed, it's only masked.

The remedy for this so-called therapeutic forgiveness-arrogance, is the forgiveness-humility that we can actually develop when we're able to ask ourselves for forgiveness, from the bottom of our heart, and when we completely let go. It's precisely this kind of humility, and this form of equanimity between self and others, that the *Forgiveness Circles* provide us with, when we all ask one another for forgiveness, gazing into each other's eyes. Or it can also be practicing *Ho'oponopono* as a group. Forgiveness is no longer abstract. Neither is it something we negotiate within us, with our conscience or the Creator. It's a very concrete action, highly personal and altogether transpersonal, that sends us back to our own humanity, and to that of each person facing us, as we belong to one single and sole humanity.

"What is magical in learning how to ask for forgiveness relies very much on the humility it allows us to recover, without which we cut ourselves off from the stream of life, love, joy and forgiveness."

So, the horizontal relationship that settles between one another, and the two-way exchanges, reopen what was shut and locked from the inside. It's in fact a very concrete process since letting go often gives way to emotional liberation (with tears) or to physical liberation (through deep muscular relaxation). All the tensions in the body and the heart can give in at last and resolve, including the intellectual tensions that come with them. Free flow is reinstated on all levels.

What's magical in learning how to ask for forgiveness relies very much on the humility it allows us to recover, without which we cut ourselves off from the stream of life, love, joy and forgiveness.

To borrow a last metaphor from *The Knight In Rusty Armour,*[4] asking for forgiveness boils down to giving up our old, rusty armour each part of which mirrors the crystallization of former judgements, former fears, and negative emotions. True, an armour protects, but its protection against blows deprives us also of the gentleness of the wind, and of caresses. It you have locked your heart, it may not be wounded any more, but it may not feel joy any more either. And this is over and above the fact that you risk hurting someone around you too, with your hands covered by your coat of mail. "Letting go of your armour" is the last image I offer you to imagine the freedom people feel when they manage to implement forgiveness both ways: in asking for forgiveness, letting it flow through us, to end up forgiving others.

[4] Robert Fisher, *The Knight in Rusty Armour* (Wiltshire Book Company, 1987).

Part 2

The Main Obstacles to Forgiveness and How to Overcome Them

To define a concept, we often need to be as specific about what it *isn't* as describing what it actually is. Why? Because we can determine in a much clearer way the limits that should not be trespassed. Explaining what something isn't is a bit like setting up barriers around what it is. Here is my home, but if you go beyond this limit, you are not on my territory anymore, you are at one of my neighbours'.

To really define what forgiveness is, as we have been trying to redefine it here, I suggest we now broach the subject of what it *isn't*, indeed what it sometimes *isn't only* when it comes under too-restrictive definitions. These confusing, erroneous or incomplete conceptions of what forgiveness really is, are as numerous obstacles that keep many of us from even taking a first step towards healing the heart.

In this chapter, as another category of obstacles to forgiveness, we will also include behaviours or beliefs, that most of us cultivate automatically or unconsciously, and that are incompatible with the practice of forgiveness. But we can learn how to become aware of them and how to change them.

This list of obstacles to forgiveness does not follow a specific order. They are given here as they appeared to me throughout the years.

1
Forgiveness Would Exclusively Be a Religious Practice

Obviously, those of you who have a regular religious practice of forgiveness will not be concerned by this first obstacle. This would be the case in Christianity, Judaism, Islam, and other religions. Nowadays, in our lay society, many people profess to no religion, indeed they have no form of spirituality, and they may even deny the very existence of such a dimension.

I was once told by a firm believer during a live radio programme in Guadeloupe, that some of those people cannot experience forgiveness because, for this woman, forgiveness could only come from above. As a consequence, if we have no link with the divine, we cannot be touched by the mercy of forgiveness, she believed.

Atheists, on the other hand, consider that forgiveness is not for them, that it's a practice only for people who follow some religion. They don't see any use for it, and they even deprecatingly consider it to fall within the province of gullibility, and incompatible with modern times. Conversely, others have the vague impression that forgiveness may possibly help them, free them, heal them, but since they see it as a religious practice, they think it will not really "work" for them, and they end up seeking elsewhere, other ways, various substitutes, that might provide them with the same liberating effect. . . which they have a hard time finding.

What about it in fact?

In fact, anyone can reach forgiveness, people who are religious, spiritual or not. I am not speculating here, nor am I putting forward a personal belief. I'm relying on the experiences of thousands of people who came, at some point, to one of the nondenominational workshops on forgiveness offered. Some of these people, though they have made the effort to attend the workshop, seriously doubt even being able to brush against the forgiveness they so long for. As a result, they're the first ones to be surprised when they acknowledge it's possible.

If forgiveness is the healing of the heart – as the metaphor of the previous chapter asserts – so this healing, just like physical healings, can be reached by anyone, regardless of their beliefs.

The real advantage there is in adhering to a religion or to a spiritual practice, is our capacity to turn to something bigger than ourselves when confronted with hardships and sufferings. If I believe in God or in any spiritual reality, I naturally leave it up to something higher than myself. In other words I naturally let go, give myself up to something that goes beyond my comprehension or even beyond me. Letting go, surrendering my mind, my certainties and my claims are precisely what allow me to reopen what was locked inside, freeing myself from my judgements, my resentment and my hatred. It's not so much the intervention of some external power – divine intercession – that gives me access to forgiveness, than my own opening, my own letting go, that allows love to spring up again, and to flow through me again. So yes, of course, if "God is love" – as many religions assert it – or if, as I sometimes like to reverse things, "love is God", when forgiveness opens me up to love again, when love flows through me again, and when it sweeps away all the emotional cholesterol obstructing my love arteries, I may, actually, have the feeling of being inspired, touched by the divine. Except that the power to open up or to lock up, that of bracing myself onto what I feel my rights are, that of laying down my arms and giving up to what is beyond me, are within me.

> "If forgiveness is the healing of the heart, so this healing,
> just like physical healings, can be reached by anyone,
> regardless of their beliefs."

Opening up, giving up or surrendering, and letting go are all as accessible to individuals who are non-believers. They only require an inner change, a capacity to turn to "higher-than-oneself" that may simply be Life or Love with a capital "L", destiny, or the order of things, whatever name we want to give it. We don't need to be believers to notice that our individual life falls within the scope of something much wider, of a tremendous web of relationships, of a whole network of causes and effects that will inevitably have an impact on our own existence. When you accept that, when you move away from the omnipotence and substitutes that some self-help techniques tend to invent, when you give up being a control-freak, when you know how to bend over without breaking, then you can develop an inner attitude that can make reopening, accepting, and the ability to humbly and wisely compromise with forces and events that are beyond us easier, instead of blocking everything and locking ourselves up for a long time in hatred and the desire for revenge. For the only control we can eventually preserve in all circumstances is the one we have on our own inner life, on our mental and emotional state, that we should methodically and patiently develop.

The most difficult thing with forgiveness, for many of us, is that it's not a matter of will – as we usually understand it – but rather of letting go, accepting. It does not trigger our active polarity, how assertive we are, how we act, how we implement our resources. It depends much more on our *receptive* polarity: accepting, receiving, integrating, letting go, surrendering. In a way, it's a kind of "feminine" dimension of our being . . . which is one of the reasons why 75% of the people attending the workshops and trainings on forgiveness are still women! For men it's all the easier to do when they are able to get in touch with their own feminine side, and when they have freed themselves from the too-often widespread illusion that letting go and accepting would be signs of weakness; that we should not let go of anything, that we should cope, and struggle. In reading the fable of the oak and the reed again, we can understand the wisdom of accepting, adapting and flexing when faced with something that goes beyond us.

Many religious and spiritual paths develop this kind of receptiveness in their followers: a capacity to open up and give up to bigger than oneself. It doesn't mean they are the only ways to reach that. Practicing martial arts like aikido or tai-chi, or sports such as surfing, sailing or dancing, can also teach those who practice them to better balance their active and receptive polarities. They end up knowing when the situation calls for acting, struggling, holding out, not giving up . . . and, on the other hand, when it's wise to accept, bend down, go with the flow, open up and allow oneself to be carried away.

Through this first obstacle to forgiveness – the illusion that religion alone can give access to it – we suddenly understand more clearly what it requires and causes within us. Forgiveness appears less as something granted us, unpredictably, from the outside, depending on God's unfathomable designs or on the vagaries of divine mercy, than it appears to be a process that requires us to act in openness, humility, letting go and accepting. In other words, when the forgiveness you want to receive is not granted, it's not that the Heavens refuse it, depending on various parameters you are not aware of. It's more often that, through clumsiness and ignorance, we ourselves block it from manifesting. There is no heart opening, because the mind shuts it, and double locks it out. We'll come back to this subject as we broach that of other obstacles to forgiveness: it's, in fact, our intellectual understanding of things, be it partial or erroneous, that shuts our heart, in a laudable but clumsy attempt to protect it, to spare it from more suffering and more wounds. On the contrary, young children whose mind is less developed, forgive easily as they are less subjected to intellectual tensions than adults.

"When the forgiveness you want to receive is not granted, it is not that the Heavens refuse it. It is more often we ourselves who block it from manifesting."

The good news is that forgiveness finally depends much more on yourself than you may think it does. Of course, it's not easy for some of us to let go, to develop the receptive polarity that makes its manifesting easier. But we can learn that, and if you want to take that path, you have several tools and methods today at your disposal to help you.

Practicing a religion or following a spiritual path may make forgiveness easier in many cases, that's for sure. However, it's not a *sine qua non* condition to implement it. Specific inner dispositions that open up to forgiveness may also be developed through other means for all the people who follow no religion or spiritual path, whether atheists, agnostics or non-believers, one way or another.

Practical Method #1

Forgive for Good:
Dr Fred Luskin's 9 Steps

Fred Luskin, Ph.D., the author of *Forgive For Good*,[5] is the director of the Stanford University Forgiveness Projects. As opposed to other approaches to forgiveness – and in particular that of Colin Tipping (see p. 76) – Luskin's is a completely lay approach, and doesn't involve adhering to any form of belief, spiritual or religious conviction. This is why I find it interesting because it can reach a wide audience that doesn't see itself as belonging to any particular denomination or philosophy.

Dr Luskin developed a 9-step process to reach forgiveness that he describes in these words on his Internet website:

1. Know exactly how you feel about what happened and be able to articulate what is not OK about the situation. Then, tell a trusted couple of people about your experience.

2. Make a commitment to yourself to do what you have to do to feel better. Forgiveness is for you and for anyone else.

3. Forgiveness does not necessarily mean reconciliation with the person that hurt you, or condoning their action. What you are after is to find peace. Forgiveness can be defined as the "peace and understanding that come from blaming that which has

---

[5] Dr Fred Luskin, Ph.D., *Forgive For Good* (HarperOne, 2003).

hurt you less, taking the life experience less personally, and changing your grievance story."

4. Get the right perspective on what is happening. Recognize that your primary distress is coming from the hurt feelings, thoughts and physical upset you are suffering now, not what offended you or hurt you two minutes – or ten years – ago. Forgiveness helps to heal those hurt feelings.

5. At the moment you feel upset, practice a simple stress management technique to soothe your body's flight or fight response.

6. Give up expecting things from other people, or your life, that they do not choose to give you. Recognize the "unenforceable rules" you have for your health or how you or other people must behave. Remind yourself that you can hope for health, love, peace and prosperity and work hard to get them.

7. Put your energy into looking for another way to get your positive goals met than through the experience that has hurt you. Instead of mentally replaying your hurt seek out new ways to get what you want.

8. Remember that a life well lived is your best revenge. Instead of focusing on your wounded feelings, and thereby giving the person who caused you pain power over you, learn to look for the love, beauty and kindness around you. Forgiveness is about personal power.

9. Amend your grievance story to remind you of the heroic choice to forgive.

As Dr Luskin says, some studies show how forgiveness contributes to significantly reducing anger, depression, and stress. His method highlights hope, peace, compassion, and self-confidence. Healthy relationships, and better physical health stem from that.

His approach has the virtue – like some others – of emphasizing our personal power, the space within us where we can find our freedom and our capacity to act. Changing the other? Most of the time, it's impossible for me. But changing how I experience things, the meaning I give them, the way I use them? Yes, I have the power to do so, provided I discover it, and know how to use it.

There is a down-to-earth, realistic, and common sense side to Luskin's method. It enables those who implement it to see life, reality, and the others as they really are, rather than as they would like them to be, and to reconcile with this reality, therefore to come to terms with it.

Those who believe in a subtle dimension, who subscribe to a religion or a spiritual path, can take it as something to build on, and can add to it a transpersonal component that will give them further access to purely personal forgiveness.

For more information, check the following website:
www.learningtoforgive.com

2

Forgiveness as Outmoded and Outdated

Following on from the first obstacle, I recall a psychotherapist who said to me, "Forgiveness is *has been*. We don't need it anymore nowadays." I've encountered this assertion in several people, in particular in those who support certain forms of psychotherapy. According to them, forgiveness belongs to the past and bears all kinds of flaws: it would be a humiliating practice, conveying a lot of guilt, and psychologically unhealthy. For them, we can manage without it today. Psychoanalysis, psychology, and various forms of psychotherapy allow individuals to do the inner work they need without having to use the outdated practice of forgiveness.

I believe this way of considering forgiveness to be altogether right *and* wrong.

I find it right if "forgiveness" means the blurry and undefined idea many of us have of it before being able to consciously clarify and deepen its meaning. Yes, I fully agree with them, there are ways of forgiving that indeed convey humiliation, guilt, and even sometimes power over others, hidden pride ("*In my great magnanimity, I will grant you forgiveness*"), not to forget self-deprecation and others. Conventional, required or mechanical forgiveness may sometimes lead to the exact opposite of what this practice should bring, as much to ourselves, actually, as to the other persons concerned. That kind of forgiveness is not therapeutical, it heals nothing. At best, it pretends. But we're only deluded for some time.

Should we therefore throw out the baby with the bathwater?

I don't believe so. Nietzsche stated "God is dead", but the death he heralded announced in fact the unavoidable death of former religious conventions, former crystallized dogmas: how dying is necessary to give birth to a new, lively, vision of spirituality, religion, and the divine. In the same way, we could also say "Forgiveness is dead":

a humiliating and shriveling forgiveness, but also, on the other end of the spectrum, the forgiveness we pour onto others, the manipulating one, the one that eases our conscience.

However, though we need to get rid of what is dead and crystallized, it's also advisable to kill that former way of forgiving, to free it from its roots, its meaning, its spirit . . . and to let it be reborn in a different way, in agreement with its time. Yes, it's true, some *forms* of forgiveness are outdated and outmoded today, considering our mentalities nowadays, even if they still agree with some of us. But the *concept* of forgiveness and the deep *meaning* of this practice are still relevant and useful.

And this is where I strongly rise up against what some psychologists today tend to do in shelving forgiveness too quickly into the boxes of the past, making no difference between content and form. Now, there are many approaches to forgiveness that are in line with our era, and with the contributions of modern psychology, whether religious (for some) or not (for others). They may perfectly well suit those for whom the former ways of forgiving are not satisfying any more.

"Yes, some forms of forgiveness are outdated and outmoded today, considering our mentalities nowadays. But the *concept* of forgiveness and the deep *meaning* of this practice are still relevant and useful."

From 2012 to 2016, after the four editions of the *Days of Forgiveness*, one of the comments we heard the most from the roughly 200 people attending this great event was: "Thank you for pulling forgiveness out of the straightjacket of religion."

I must say I'm very respectful of religious traditions, and representatives of Christianity and Buddhism in particular were invited to attend this event. They actually made remarkable and noted speeches. What the people attending told us was that basically, thanks to the multiple lectures, workshops, and ceremonies offered, they were able to revise and enlarge their definition of forgiveness, and to learn, at the same time, new rituals and new methods to implement it.

Forgiveness – like love, truth, freedom etc. – is not a static, unchanging notion, eternally frozen in its definition and practice. From one religion to another, from one civilization to another, from times past to modern times, its understanding has evolved, its implementation has been transformed, and this is going to continue in the same way. Challenging this concept may be done collectively, at times when society, as a whole, evolves, as well as individually. Each one of us is entirely free to question these notions, to go deeply into them, to turn them over in their mind, to experience them, to implement them, and to make them their own. It's not only up to theologians, philosophers or experts. As we can see with the success of philosophy taught to young children, there is no age to start asking ourselves deep questions, and to start finding our own answers, enlightened by those given by former generations.

Do you find such a practice of forgiveness outdated, outmoded, *has been*, or incompatible with your mentality, your view on things, your own philosophy?

OK!

So, roll up your sleeves, and tackle this question seriously, in all awareness. Read several books. Think about it. Go deeper into it. What is forgiveness, basically? Its etymology, its meaning? What do various traditions or thinkers say about it? And what do I think about it? How do I see it? How can I make it my own? . . .

This is where it becomes interesting!

And I really wish this book, and in particular this part in which we explain in detail the obstacles to forgiveness – relying on former notions that it's high time we question – may help you reach your own understanding of forgiveness, to then savour its therapeutic and freeing effects in *your own* life.

♡

Laure's Testimony

"During the presentation of the *Gift of Forgiveness* workshop, I became aware of the fact that I was missing a key to truly implement forgiveness, and this key was . . . myself. Until then, I had been sort of nonexistent when I forgave. To my mind, only the other person existed, I had to forgive the other person at all costs, and in the end, despite my efforts, it was difficult for me to forgive.

"With the *Gift of Forgiveness*, you're in the very heart of this dynamic, because forgiving is an act of Love towards yourself. You reconnect with this powerful, warm, and harmonious energy of Love. It flows within you again. And when I felt it flowing again, I started sobbing uncontrollably. I was freeing myself, and at the same time I felt a renewed joy at being reconnected, I recovered my identity.

"I had just received a unique, grandiose, and deeply touching gift, and I couldn't keep it to myself, like a hidden treasure. I felt the need to share it.

"So I trained to be able to to transmit it to others. Since then, once a month, I experience this unique moment with people attending, for each circle is different, but the energy of Love is always there, and it's powerful. There is an alchemy that occurs between the place and the people participating. It's very moving to see the wisdom of the heart expressing itself. And all of this happens in a very natural and simple way. While lulled by, and surrounded with, the energy of Love, we each experience our inner path towards Forgiveness. Awareness awakens, eyes light up, and that's when my heart overflows with gratitude and thankfulness."

♡

3

Forgiveness Would Mainly Be a Gift to the Other

Could believing that be an obstacle? For many people, yes. Why?

Because if I believe that granting forgiveness to someone who hurt me, and for whom I still hold a grudge, is a gift to that person, an inner voice will immediately arise to say, "NO, no way! I'm not making him or her that gift! I was hurt, I suffered a lot, so don't count on me to grant forgiveness." In thinking that way, I'm convinced I'm punishing the other by refusing forgiveness. I believe it's that person who will suffer now.

Is this a fair way to see things?

Actually, not really. In fact, not at all.

If I am physically attacked and wounded, not taking care of myself will make *me* suffer first. If the other person has a change of mind, that person might also be affected. But they may also not care less, or may never know about it. In the same way, if my heart was hurt, if I suffered things that deeply affected me in my emotional integrity (not the physical one), refusing to heal – which means refusing to grant forgiveness since forgiveness is described here as healing the wounds of the heart– is mainly going to make *me* suffer. I'm the one who will go on poisoning myself with hatred, resentment, and the desire for revenge. I'm the one who will spend months, years, maybe decades, with open and painful wounds in my emotional body. I'm the one who will have a wounded heart, emotional cysts, and an emotional handicap.

Will the person who hurt me suffer from my refusal to grant forgiveness? Not sure. It varies a lot from one person to another. While some would like to be forgiven their wrongs one day, others really don't care. However, it's true that from a spiritual point of view, my hatred – which is a negative energy though an invisible one – will do no good to the person to whom I send it. It's a kind of psychological attack that may sometimes have tangible effects. Except that by going through me first before reaching its goal, I would be the one to have to pay the most for it. Secondly, it will inevitably have an effect on all of my other relationships, including those I am closest to, who would also, indirectly, pay the highest price. Because yes, the human heart is one, and if it exudes hatred on one side, it cannot box itself off and express pure and unstained love on the other side. Thirdly, all the negative energy I express – just like everything I sow with my thoughts, my intentions and my feelings – is going to attract similar energies to me, therefore negative ones too, and I risk locking myself into an infernal vicious circle.

Do I really want that? No, obviously not. And most of us fall into that trap out of sheer ignorance of its mechanics and consequences.

The best way to avoid this obstacle is precisely to be aware of the fact that forgiveness is first and foremost something we do *for ourselves*! We forgive to free ourselves from the poison of hatred, to heal our own wounds, to cure our own heart. We forgive in order not to remain crippled in our heart and unable to love again fully, even those who are closest.

"Forgiveness is first and foremost something we do *for ourselves*! We forgive to free ourselves from the poison of hatred, to heal our own wounds, to cure our own heart."

What's difficult here lies in the fact that resentment is a link. In French, there is in fact the expression, *Je t'en veux* – unknown in other languages – that I find very expressive. It literally means *I use my will on you*. It means *I have a hold on you* through a link of resentment and hatred. I don't want to let you go because of what you've done to me. If I ever for-*gave* you, I'd relinquish this link, I'd free you . . . No way! So I continue to hold it against you, and the link of resentment I cultivate chains me to you, therefore limits me. To get rid of this link, to be able heal oneself, it's necessary to make the distinction between two levels, two dimensions within us that we tend to confuse and mix up: our heart and our mind. As we'll go deeper into this matter later, implementing forgiveness (healing our heart) does not mean becoming an idiot intellectually and making stupid decisions. I can forgive... and bring a legal charge against someone. "I forgive everything . . . but I leave nothing out!", said one of my spiritual mentors. "I forgive everything" means "I refuse to poison myself with the venom of hatred, so I do what's necessary to heal my heart." And "leaving nothing out" means "I also don't lack judgement and common sense. I know that what you've done is unacceptable. So, without hatred, I do what is needed so that you're confronted with the consequences of your actions."

I'll go deeper into this main subject later. What's important for you to understand, while tackling this specific obstacle, is that you can forgive, you can *make* this *gift to yourself*, grant yourself the healing of your emotional wounds, without necessarily freeing the others – those who hurt you – from the legal consequences of their actions. Yes, you free them from your hatred, since you're the first one to get something out of it. But you don't necessarily give the others a blank check that would shield them from all responsibility. So, you must make the difference between two important things to protect yourself from this obstacle:

- a first difference between how we act towards ourselves, and towards the others: what do I plan to do for myself, to heal myself, to recover my integrity? And what will I do towards the person who did me wrong? These are two very different things, that you must deal with separately, making the distinction between them. The choice is not between "I suffer to make the other suffer" or "I heal, but in the process I free the other." There is a third way to deal with this: "I heal, I take care of myself . . . but I keep a free hand on acting towards the other as required by the wrong committed."

- a second difference between what happens in my heart, and in my mind: instead of the two working together (either negatively "I don't forget and I condemn", or positively "I forgive and accept"), I develop their respective autonomy: my heart forgives, heals, and recovers its integrity and flow, while my mind keeps all its ability to judge and makes the fair decisions that are required to protect my heart, and puts the people concerned in front of their responsibility. We shall see that this is the condition for the inner couple "heart/mind" to take their full space instead of alternatively submitting one to the other while our decisions err one way or the other.

Once this third obstacle is put aside, the word forgiveness should automatically mean something that does *you* good! The centre of gravity of this word would stop being on the same level as the other person, what that person says or does, what that person deserves or not, to reposition it on ourself: how do I want to live? What state do I want to be in? How can I heal?

Once I've healed myself, the decisions I make concerning the others are not dictated by my hatred or resentment anymore: they can therefore be more objective and fairer, because they come from a space within me that has calmed down.

Bear this in mind: when you forgive, you are first and foremost freeing yourself. The opposite, *holding* a grudge, is a dangerous form of emotional constipation. Would forgiveness be an emotional laxative? Here is an unexpected metaphor, though very significant, to add to the others!

The Forgiveness Project
The Story of Bud Welch (USA)

I have to do something different,
because what I'm doing isn't working.

In April 1995 Bud Welch's 23-year-old daughter, Julie Marie, was killed in the bombing of the Murrah Federal Building in Oklahoma City along with 167 others. In the months after her death, Bud changed from supporting the death penalty for Timothy McVeigh and Terry Nichols to taking a public stand against it. In 2001 Timothy McVeigh was executed for his part in the bombing.

"Three days after the bombing, as I watched Tim McVeigh being led out of the courthouse, I hoped someone in a high building with a rifle would shoot him dead. I wanted him to fry. In fact, I'd have killed him myself if I'd had the chance.

Unable to deal with the pain of Julie's death, I started self-medicating with alcohol until eventually the hangovers were lasting all day. Then, on a cold day in January 1996, I came to the bomb site – as I did every day – and I looked across the wasteland where the Murrah Building once stood. My head was splitting from drinking the night before and I thought, 'I have to do something different, because what I'm doing isn't working.'

"For the next few weeks I started to reconcile things in my mind, and finally concluded that it was revenge and hate that had killed Julie and the 167 others. Tim McVeigh and Terry Nichols had been against the US government for what happened in Waco, Texas, in 1993, and seeing what they'd done with their vengeance, I knew I had to send mine in a different direction. Shortly afterwards I started speaking out against the death penalty.

"I also remembered that shortly after the bombing I'd seen a news report on Tim McVeigh's father, Bill. He was shown stooping over a flowerbed, and when he stood up I could see that he'd been physically bent over in pain. I recognized it because I was feeling that pain, too.

"In December 1998, after Tim McVeigh had been sentenced to death, I had a chance to meet Bill McVeigh at his home near Buffalo. I wanted to show him that I did not blame him. His youngest daughter, Jennifer, also wanted to meet me, and after Bill had showed me his garden, the three of us sat around the kitchen table.

"Up on the wall were family snapshots, including Tim's graduation picture. They noticed that I kept looking up at it, so I felt compelled to say something. 'God, what a good-looking kid,' I said.

"Earlier, when we'd been in the garden, Bill had asked me, 'Bud, are you able to cry?' I'd told him, 'I don't usually have a problem crying.' His reply was, 'I can't cry, even though I've got a lot to cry about.' But now, sitting at the kitchen table, looking at Tim's photo, a big tear rolled down his face. It was the love of a father for a son.

"When I got ready to leave, I shook Bill's hand, then extended it to Jennifer, but she just grabbed me and threw her arms around me. She was the same sort of age as Julie but felt so much taller. I don't know which one of us started crying first. Then I held her face in my hands and said, 'Look, honey, the three of us are in this for the rest of our lives. I don't want your brother to die and I'll do everything I can to prevent it.'

"As I walked away from the house, I realized that until that moment I had walked alone, but now a tremendous weight had lifted from my shoulders. I had found someone who was a bigger victim of the Oklahoma bombing than I was, because while I can speak in front of thousands of people and say wonderful things about Julie, if Bill McVeigh meets a stranger he probably doesn't even say he had a son.

"About a year before the execution I found it in my heart to forgive Tim McVeigh. It was a release for me rather than for him.

"Six months after the bombing a poll taken in Oklahoma City of victims' families and survivors showed that 85 per cent wanted the death penalty for Tim McVeigh. Six years later that figure had dropped to nearly half, and now most of those who supported his execution have come to believe it was a mistake. In other words, they didn't feel any better after Tim McVeigh was taken from his cell and killed."

4

Forgiving Would Amount to Condoning, Accepting, and Excusing

H ere we are broaching one of the most widespread obstacles to forgiveness. Many people think "If I forgive, it means I condone what was done to me, that it was acceptable. No way!" Isn't this a very understandable reaction?

But who says these two ideas necessarily go hand in hand?

Once more, we are deluded by the lack of distinction – which most of us have grown up with – between what happens within our heart and within our mind, between our feelings and emotions on the one hand, and our sense of discrimination, our judgements on the other hand.

When I believe that "if I forgive, then I condone", it means my heart and my mind have merged into a single entity, with two possible consequences:

- either my heart and my emotions reduce my mind to justifying what I feel (and to refrain from any thought that does not go the same way)

- or, quite the opposite, it's my mind that governs my heart, it's my intellectual constructions and my way of interpreting the situation that tell my emotions what to nourish (or to ban).

So, if my heart forgives, my mind feels compelled at the same time to condone the wrong done. As a matter of fact, we can learn to listen to the different echoes of these two parts of ourselves, without stifling the one or the other, and without letting one of them dictate the other's behaviour. There is an analogy that can help us reach that.

Look at how things unfold in court. On one side, there is the prosecutor who coldly and objectively lists the facts the accused is blamed for. And on the other side, there is the lawyer who tries to sensitize the audience to his client's life, to touch the jury's hearts by trying to make them understand things as seen from the inside, subjectively speaking. In the middle, there is the judge who will have to make the final decision. Within us, the prosecutor is our mind: it's the side of us that sees things from the outside, and tries to be objective. The lawyer is our heart: its language is that of feelings, it's here to stir us. The lawyer and the prosecutor each have their own role, their own understanding of the situation. It's in combining the two that the judge can make a fair decision (based on the jury's decision).

In the same way, I can implement forgiveness to heal my heart, to free myself from hatred, to live again, and at the same time I can continue, objectively, to consider the wrong done as totally unacceptable and blameworthy. For myself, I forgive, and I heal. For the other, I am capable of discernment and, if needed, I can even seek cause of action. Forgiving does not make me stupid, nor does it make me inconsequent.

"For myself, I forgive, and I heal. For the other, I am capable of discernment and, if needed, I can even seek cause of action. Forgiving does not make me stupid, nor does it make me inconsequent."

Who, as a parent, has never been confronted with their child after they had done something foolish or wrong, and has not felt a surge from the heart to forgive while at the same time the rational need to punish the child despite it?

Forgiveness and love do not prevent punishment, I would even say it is the highest form of love one can show his child. A brave love, not a weak one that might harm the child. In the same way, just as you can forgive a child without condoning his wrongdoing nor depriving him of its consequences, you can also develop the same ability to act faced with the injustices you have, yourself, been subjected to, even if this proves difficult, and requires time and training.

Let's now deal with the verb "excuse". Forgiving is not excusing. In the lines above, I opposed forgiving to holding a grudge. In the same way, excusing can be opposed to accusing. I can forgive while retaining my accusations. For myself, I hold onto no grudge, I don't remain in hatred but it doesn't prevent me from still assessing, objectively and severely, the action committed against me. I don't excuse it. At least, not necessarily. I can find that my aggressors had reasons for doing that: their story, childhood, what they had undergone, and so forth. But a reason is not an excuse. All of those who have had the same childhood, who have undergone the same hardships, haven't all become like that person who did me wrong. Far from it. I can understand without approving. I can forgive without excusing.

In common language, the verbs "forgive" and "excuse" are often used one for the other, thus this confusion. We tend to ask children to excuse themselves, so they immediately whisper sheepishly "forgive me". In fact, these are very different things. When I excuse someone, it means I hold no charge anymore against that person. When I forgive, it means I stop hating or holding a grudge against that person. These notions are on two different levels.

"When I excuse someone, it means I hold no charge anymore against that person. When I forgive, it means I stop hating or holding a grudge against that person. These notions are on two different levels."

By the way, you may note that excusing oneself ("excuse me") is a somewhat questionable practice. Can you imagine, in the same way, someone who would say to you, "I excuse myself"?! It's much better to offer one's apologies, that the other is free to accept or not. Apologizing is admitting one's mistakes. In expressing this acknowledgment, we allow the other to decide on how to react, to excuse or not, to forgive or not, to excuse without forgiving, etc.

Practicing forgiveness therefore requires a much keener awareness of what's going on within us, and in particular distinguishing more accurately what's going on in our mind, in our heart and also in our body. This distinction will then very naturally be reflected in the vocabulary we choose to express ourselves: the heart forgives or not, the mind excuses or not, the body accepts or not. We are lucky to have a very rich language but it takes learning inside how to use all the subtle nuances the richness of our vocabulary allows us to express.

Bear in mind, from what has just been said, that you can absolutely forgive without having to accept, support or excuse wrongs that you find unacceptable and inexcusable.

The Forgiveness Project
The Story of Andrew Rice (USA)

Those people crying loudest for retribution
so often seem to be the least affected.

On September 11, 2001, investment banker David Rice was killed when the World Trade Center collapsed. Since then, his younger brother, Andrew Rice, has dedicated himself to trying to understand the underlying causes of violence. Andrew is a member of Peaceful Tomorrows, a group founded by family members of September 11 victims seeking effective non-violent responses to terrorism.

"I was covering the Toronto Film Festival as a journalist on September 11. It was a bright sunny morning when my mum rang. 'Andrew, are you alone?' she asked, and a kind of dread came over me. She told me David had rung to tell her that a plane had hit the World Trade Center but that he was OK: it had hit the other tower.

"I rushed to the press room of my hotel and as I walked in I saw the second jet hit. I was hysterical now and ran back to my hotel suite. I turned on the TV to catch the first tower collapsing. At this point I just let out this terrible shriek, overwhelmed by the certainty that David was dead.

"David and I were always close. As teenagers we were both wild – we dropped out of college and partied too much until our twenties, when we both sobered up. The process of sobering up makes you face yourself and makes you understand that everyone has good and bad in them. When David was killed it helped me to handle my grief and anger.

"When the New York Times published its 'Portrait of Grief' of David, I was too distressed to take it in, but some months later I looked at the newspaper again and was shocked that in that same edition – just six days after the attacks – Vice President Cheney was saying, 'If you're against us you'll feel our wrath.' The nation was in shock, like clay waiting to be molded, and here were our leaders saying we would rid the world of evil. There was a battle going on inside me – the visceral part was saying 'we'll show them', but the more rational part was saying 'force won't help'. Then, as reports of civilian casualties came in from Afghanistan, I found myself getting more and more upset that ordinary people like my brother were losing their lives. When I discovered Peaceful Tomorrows on the Internet, it was a huge relief to realize I wasn't the only one who thought retribution would get us nowhere.

"Later, a group called Murder Victims Families for Reconciliation were contacted by the mother of the alleged 20th hijacker, Zacharias Moussaoui, who has been held in solitary confinement in Northern Virginia since September 11. She had a unique request. She wanted to meet some of the families of the victims and ask for their forgiveness.

"We were nervous; scared of our Government finding out, and scared it would be just too upsetting. But finally a small group of us agreed to meet Madame al-Wafi in New York City in November 2002. As we waited in a private university building, a mother whose son was killed in the World Trade Center went down the hall to meet her. We heard footsteps, then silence. Then we heard this sobbing. Finally they both came into the room, both mothers with their arms around each other. By now we were all crying. Madame al-Wafi reminded me a lot of my own mother, who had cried so much after David died. She spent three hours with us and told us how the extremist group had given her mentally ill son a purpose in life.

"One day I'd like to meet Zacharias Moussaoui. I'd like to say to him, 'You can hate me and my brother as much as you like, but I want you to know that I loved your mother and I comforted her when she was crying.'

"My attitude is not all altruism. Of course I'm angry, but there's a spiritual supremacy. I'm protecting my brother's spirit by putting a barricade around him. I'm refusing to fall in line with what 'they' want, which is visceral hatred between two sides; this gives me permission to reconcile. Those people crying loudest for retribution so often seem to be the least affected."

5

Forgiving Would Be Impossible without the Other Offering Their Apologies or Asking for Forgiveness

---

Some say, "I cannot forgive someone who has not asked for it." This posture, that may seem logical in the standard understanding of what forgiveness is, is in fact a great hindrance to the "healing of the heart" we have been dealing with here.

As long as I wait for the ones who wronged me to come offer their apologies and/or ask for forgiveness, I remain helpless, and passive: the power to heal, to reawaken to love, lies in the hands of my wrongdoers. If they don't acknowledge their wrongs, if they're not aware of the harm they caused me, if they just don't care, if they live on the other side of the planet and I never see them, or even if they had the bad idea of dying without having ever asked me for forgiveness nor having offered their excuses, am I then sentenced to spend the rest of my life suffering, without finding peace in my heart, without being able to heal and love again? Is that our human condition?

To use another analogy, imagine you've gone for a walk in a disreputable neighbourhood in town, and that someone has attacked you, and stabbed you. You are bleeding, you need care. Now, imagine that to cure and to heal, it has to be your aggressor himself who disinfects, bandages, and maybe even stiches up again your wound! What a mess we would all be in if that were the only way to cure our physical wounds!? It's a blessing that, for minor wounds, we can all cure ourselves and, if they are more serious, we can go see a nurse or a doctor.

It's the same with emotional wounds, those that have nothing to do with our physical body but with our heart, our emotional body.

Their healing is not within the hands of our aggressors. For most of them, we can heal ourself, and today there are many approaches to implement healing our heart's wounds. For the most serious ones, there are also people to help us, resource persons, Counsellors, workshops or retreats, to lead us onto the path to healing.

Of course, if the person who attacked or wounded us comes to offer excuses, if that person makes amends, if that person even goes so far as to ask for forgiveness and tries to repair, it's great, it's marvellous, it's the ideal situation! No-one can dispute this, and I will certainly not dispute it. We all dream of that. It's the perfect situation with forgiveness, repair, reconciliation: the whole thing. But is it always possible? No. Very often, there are many factors out of our range that don't help. The other doesn't want to fill in his/her part of the contract with us, or can't.

In such situations, it's vital to know that you can heal *yourself* anyway. Your healing doesn't depend on what the others say or don't say, on what the others do or don't do. It only depends on you. Can you imagine all the difference that makes? A great one! I used to think the others held power over me, that only their attitude would determine whether I could reach forgiveness or not. And I realize now that I have this power, that the others only had it insofar as I was giving it up to them myself! It's a wonderful reversal!

"I used to think the others held power over me,
that only their attitude would determine whether I could
encounter forgiveness or not. And I realize now that I have
this power, that the others only had it insofar
as I was giving it up to them myself!"

This is what makes one of the people quoted on the *Forgiveness Project* website say: "Forgiveness is the ultimate form of revenge: you deprive the other of the power he/she thought they had on you." Obviously, this is a paradoxical joke: forgiveness as the ultimate form of revenge.

However, what I like in this quotation – that can be credited with racking our brains – is that it forces us to examine the situation from an unexpected point of view. I saw myself as the powerless victim of others, while in fact I had a power I couldn't see, that I thought was in the hands of others.

This paradoxical sentence also brings to light the fact that, as long as I cannot forgive, I actually give my aggressor all power, I extend in the long-term the wrong I suffered a few weeks, months or years ago. To repeat the analogy already mentioned with a physical wound: that person really hurt me at some time in the past, but since then, I have unknowingly prevented my wounds to heal by ignoring my own resources.

Becoming aware of the part we play ourselves in perpetuating our own sufferings, is giving ourselves the means to heal them. It means changing our centre of gravity: not focusing on the others anymore, on what they said or did, on what they could do for us if only they accepted or acknowledged their wrongs, to refocus instead on ourselves, on our own resources, our own capacity to heal. In an interview she granted the magazine *Paris Match* in 2014 about a new book, Ingrid Betancourt – former candidate to the Presidency of Colombia, held captive during five years by the Colombian Revolutionary Armed Forces – stressed the idea of reversing attitudes that forgiveness often implies. She wrote, "Without taking the path to forgiveness, we not only deny the other's humanity in its darkness, but also our own. For what is unforgivable? It's not the wrong done to us, it's our fury for having put ourselves in such a painful situation. Forgiveness *doesn't act on the other, it's on our own ego* [I'm the one stressing this]. When we forgive something, it's making peace with ourselves."

In conclusion, don't let the past behaviour of those who hurt you still determine today whether or not you can reach forgiveness and peace of heart. They're not the ones to decide, you are. You can make the choice to heal, whatever they do or don't do. And if, fortunately, they in turn take a step towards you, if they walk half the way, it will be a gift, a bonus. You will not have waited for their gesture to recover the integrity of your heart and your own capacity to love.

Ingrid Betancourt also said that "Forgiveness is essential to live. Without it, without this spiritual behaviour, we never return to human relationships with others." And we could add: neither with ourselves. So, let the others choose their acts, since you have no way of forcing them to act one way or another, and since only asking for forgiveness or genuine excuses have some value. Just concentrate on your own latitude for freedom and responsibility: heal your wounds to recover a loving heart and truly human relationships with everyone and with yourself.

Practical Method #2

Colin Tipping's Radical Forgiveness

Colin Tipping's approach to forgiveness, through his books and in the workshops he leads in many countries, comes from his work with people who are at the end of their lives. The idea of short-term death brings many people to want to "sort out their lives" as we would say, and more particularly to free themselves from the burden of resentment, or situations that have not yet been settled as they reach the end of their lives. They want to die peacefully.

With little time ahead of them – a few months, sometimes a few weeks – there is no time to beat around the bush, nor is there time to dilute the job or to delay. If forgiveness is to be, then it's now or never.

Colin Tipping uses the constraint of time as an asset. Indeed, it actually allows him to introduce his audience to a more *radical* approach to forgiveness, that many people would not be ready to consider or accept under normal circumstances. I would like to point out that today the Tipping method is taught to all kinds of people, not only people approaching the end of their lives.

The key to this radical approach lies in the fact that Tipping invites his readers to believe that *nothing unfair ever happens to you.* In other words, even the most painful events you have encountered in your life are part and parcel of your life mission or your "soul contract". Seen from this perspective, nothing has happened to you out of bad luck or by accident. Everything has a meaning, even if it is hard to see, and if your ego is often incapable of understanding it, and even if these hardships recall very painful emotions.

Therefore, according to Tipping, if everything has a meaning, if nothing unfair has ever happened to us, there is nothing to forgive either. I need to forgive you only if I still hold a grudge against you, if I judge you, if I consider that whatever happened to me should never have happened, in other words if I'm in conflict with what life imposes on me. If, on the contrary, thanks to a reversal of comprehension, I end up understanding and accepting everything that has happened to me, including the most dramatic events, then I let go. I stop struggling against my own life or rejecting it, I accept it. Thus, in giving up the heavy burden of accusations – against others, against myself, against Life or God – that I was bearing, it's the very need to forgive that disappears with it, because there is no need for it anymore.

Believing that is not easy to accept for everyone, and in some ways, it's close to various Eastern notions in relation to karma. It's actually totally unacceptable for many people, in particular in our modern Western culture that stresses the individual, free will, and the ability to control one's own life with no god and no master. Yet, it echoes some of the works of very trendy authors nowadays such as don Miguel Ruiz. In his book *Beyond Fear: A Toltec Guide to Freedom and Joy,* he writes about how he had the same revelation one day in Teotihuacan (Mexico): nothing unfair happens in the world. (See Recommended Reading, p. 151)

Understanding such a conception of things requires going very deeply into the notions of justice and injustice, until one is able to see that some apparent "injustices", on a human level, actually serve a higher justice that goes beyond our understanding, and occurs within the very injustices we think we can detect. Going deeper into this issue would go beyond the subject of this book, but I encourage all of those interested to try it: beyond the help it could bring to implement forgiveness in a radical way, reflecting on this issue can bring a different outlook on what's happening in our collective and individual lives.

In concrete terms, practicing radical forgiveness is going to include the following four great steps (on Colin Tipping's website, there is a very detailed worksheet to apply this process to one's own hardships):

1. **Telling the Story** – This is where we describe in detail the situation that caused a problem, the tragedy we underwent. This first tale is generally told from the viewpoint of the victim, stressing the painful feelings felt, because of someone else.

2. **Feeling the Feelings** – In this second step, people accept feeling emotions. During a workshop, those people may externalize them (Colin Tipping sometimes uses a tennis racket and big cushions so people can vent their anger and fury). The individuals become aware of the fact that these emotions are their own: "No one can make me feel anything", says the worksheet. In other words, my perception and comprehension of things are what make me feel such-and-such emotion.

3. **Collapsing the Story** – It's in this third step that a reversal of situation occurs. The idea is to accept that the painful event we were reproaching our aggressor with, was part of our life track. At the same time, with it we become aware of the fact that our inner state, according to Tipping, is mostly due to our own denial, our refusal of the situation, through our struggle against "what is", therefore what happened to us.

4. **Reframing the Story** – "I now realize that what I was going through (my Victim Story), perfectly reflected my limited (Human) perception of the situation. I understand that I can now change this reality by simply being willing to see the perfection in this situation." This is what the worksheet states at the beginning of this last step, whose goal is to reconcile individuals with what they've gone through, to make them attempt a different understanding of the same event (a reframe), a new "non-victim" story, to lead them towards a forgiveness that encompasses the other as well as themselves.

Tipping's approach deserves credit for allowing us to discover the only space of freedom that we can never be deprived of, the one left when there is no more hope: transforming our own perception of what we experienced and, at the same time, transforming the emotions that event has caused. As Ingrid Betancourt said, what we cannot forgive "is not the wrong done to us, it's our fury for having put ourselves in such a painful situation. Forgiveness doesn't act on the other, it's on our own ego." It's our ego's struggle against reality that creates an armour or a shield around us, behind which no forgiveness is possible. And it's precisely this denial, this refusal of the reality, this gap with our own life, that the Tipping method can allow to repair and change, just because it is *radical*.

And because it's a radical approach, it really is a suitable method for people who are themselves in a similarly radical or extreme situation, whether it's the end of their life, or confronting events that are so completely out of their control that they can only deal with them through surrendering and accepting, so that they can draw something precious from it. It can also be suitable for anyone who can easily go from one extreme to another, who can experience inner reversals at 180°, or for whoever likes changes and is not satisfied with half-measures.

For more information, check this website:
www.radicalforgiveness.com

6

If We Have Forgiven,
We Should Forget

The issue of the fair balance between forgetting and forgiving has been the subject of many debates, and has caused very contradictory answers in which we don't all necessarily find our bearings.

For some of us – as suggested by the title of this sixth obstacle – once we have forgiven, we should forget. In English, these two verbs are similar and often used together: forgive and forget. For those who support this position, if we don't forget, it means we haven't really forgiven. It means there are still some grudges, unresolved things. Others refuse this solution that seems unbearable or unfair to them. They agree to forgive, but certainly not to forget.

There are two examples that illustrate these two stances. Though one is well-known, the other isn't.

Since the Shoah, children at school are taught the "duty to remember". To never forget what happened, what the Nazis inflicted on the Jews. There is a main risk in choosing this option which is to fuel, in a certain sense forever, past wounds, and to never allow their full and permanent healing.

By contrast, in the north of California, there is an American Indian tribe called the Yuroks. For them, the duty to forget is of greater, if not, paramount importance. Indeed, when a serious offence or a crime is committed, followed by acknowledgement and repair, it is strictly forbidden to mention it again. Mentioning it again is considered a crime as serious as murder. It amounts to symbolically digging up the dead.

So, do we need to remember or do we need to forget?

There is a very wise Jewish saying that goes "Between two solutions, choose the third one." The third one here consists in knowing what to recall and what to forget. Here, we also need to use judgement and subtlety. To use another analogy, let's take a look at the distillation of an aromatic plant in a still: thyme, sage, rosemary, as you wish. This plant is composed of parts that go bad and rot. But there are also components that can keep for a long time. On the one hand, there is the vegetable matter, the stems, the leaves, the flowers, etc. This matter, symbolically speaking, is the painful event we have experienced, the distinctive and unique shape it took on. On the other hand, there is the aromatic quintessence within this matter, the spirit of the plant, or the lessons we can distil with it to create an essential oil. It's the live meaning of the event, the one that can durably be preserved, and can release at any time its fragrance, its message. It also has therapeutic virtues. After distillation, the aromatic matter is thrown away or burned: we only keep the essential oil produced in this way.

In other words, faced with the painful events of our individual or collective lives, we can choose to distil their lessons, their quintessence, and at the same time let forgetting do its job on the specific aspect they had at the time, in that context. Forgetting the quintessence, or the lessons we were taught by one event or another, would be a mistake. But keeping a dead, half-rotten plant, is no better.

Let's go further. This quintessence does not only concern one specimen of a specific plant – rosemary or sage – but all of those of the same species, even if their outer appearance may greatly vary from one plant to another. To say it differently, the lesson I distilled from a unique event can apply in the same way to thousands of others. Therefore, though it's highly pertinent but still very restricted, I don't only retain from that story the fact that one should not attack Jews. Beyond this particular case, the essence of which I extracted, I understand that nothing can justify attacking another human being, whatever their religion, nationality, ethnical origins or race.

The news bitterly shows how little we have retained from history, maybe precisely because its particular shapes have been fossilized, without taking the trouble to distil its meaningful seeds to sow them into the mind of each child. "We cannot carry an oakwood with us," Omraam Mikhaël Aïvanhov used to say, "but we can carry a bag of acorns with us." Factual history, with its dates to learn by heart, is the oakwood. Its lessons are the universal principles we can draw from, it's the bag of acorns.

So, to get back to forgiveness, you can altogether forgive, forget one day the specific details of one painful situation or another that you experienced, while recalling the general conclusions you drew from them, that you can apply to many similar situations. This will enable you to live more lightly (with no oaks to bear), while retaining the essential part of what you experienced, the quintessence of what you will have patiently distilled from your life experiences, including the most difficult ones.

Besides, it's the example nature itself shows, in rejecting and recycling old forms while indefinitely preserving the vital information they bear within them in the shape of DNA. Retain information (rather than a grudge), remember the lessons, and let time allow the shape and texture of events to be forgotten. The path to forgiveness will thus be easier to take, with no useless burden, but no misplaced amnesia either.

The Forgiveness Project
The Story of Katy Hutchison & Ryan Aldridge (Canada)

Whether victim or perpetrator, part of being human is rolling up our sleeves and taking an active part in repairing harm.

On New Year's Eve 1997, Katy Hutchison's husband, Bob, was beaten to death while checking on a party being thrown by his neighbour's son. In the small town of Squamish in British Columbia, a wall of silence soon grew up around the murder. It was four years before Ryan Aldridge acknowledged having delivered the fatal blow. He was convicted of manslaughter and sentenced to five years in prison.

Katy Hutchison

"Less than an hour after Bob was murdered, I stood in the emergency ward beside his body, overwhelmed by a sense of peace, knowing that wherever Bob was now, it was much safer than the place he had just been. Then I went home to tell my four-year-old twins, Amelia and Sam, that their Daddy was dead. I looked into their eyes and knew that I could not allow their lives to become dominated by their father's death. I promised them and I promised myself that underneath the horror of what had just happened we would find a gift.

"As for the rest of the community, the code of silence began that night. No one called the police, no one spoke out. The murder was devastating, but the silence from so many compounded the devastation. In the end, I chose to leave my community and return to the community I had grown up in.

"Eventually, after four years, Ryan Aldridge was arrested. That same day, as I was leaving the police station, I spotted him on camera, alone in the investigation room. The police had left the tape rolling and I stood and watched him falling apart. I didn't want to leave him.

"After his arrest, police officers showed Ryan a video I'd made urging him to dig down deep to find the words to say, 'I did this.' Four years of silence, grief and fear then fell away as he fulfilled my wish and confessed to the crime. Those words would begin the healing process for both of us. He then stunned police by asking to meet me, and so, less than 24 hours after his arrest, I found myself face-to-face with the man who had murdered my husband. As he sobbed it was all I could do not to hold him. *Second to the day I gave birth, it was probably the most human moment of my life.*

"Sometime into Ryan's sentence I discovered an incredible organization called Community Justice Initiatives that was able to organize a Victim-Offender Reconciliation between Ryan and I. It took place in the prison and lasted most of the day: we spoke about almost everything – our lives, our hobbies, our families. There were tears, there were long silences where neither of us had the words to fill the space. In that meeting I told Ryan that I had forgiven him.

"I've been able to forgive Ryan because of the immense sympathy I have for his mother. I understood her loss. We haven't met yet but we write and I cherish her letters. Forgiveness isn't easy. Taking tranquillizers and having someone look after your kids would probably be easier, but I feel compelled to do something with Bob's legacy. I want to tell my story to help change people's perceptions – and where possible I want to do this with Ryan by my side. I'll never understand how our universes collided – but they did, and as Bob can't make a further contribution to society, then perhaps Ryan can.

"Whether victim or perpetrator, part of being human is rolling up our sleeves and taking an active part in repairing harm.

"Amelia and Sam have fully supported my choice to forgive Ryan, but others have asked, 'How could you?' The way I saw it how could I not? My children had lost their father and I did not want them to lose me in the process. If I had been consumed by hatred, anger and vengeance, what kind of mother would I be? Something happened when Bob died and I found my voice. Forgiveness became an opportunity to create a new and hopeful beginning.

"Looking back 17 years, I realize how dynamic the forgiveness experience has been. It changes shape; some days growing, others withering. It is heart work of the highest order. I am thankful to Ryan for making the very best of his life, moving forward and working hard to care for his family and contribute to his community. But mostly I remain grateful for the brave hearts of my now-adult children and my second husband Michael, who supported my choice and trusted me on this uncharted journey of the heart."

Ryan Aldridge

"Katy's forgiveness is the most incredible thing that anyone has ever given me. It changed my life. There's trouble every day in prison, offers of drugs and threats of fights, but I don't give in. My life would still be full of anger and violence if it wasn't for Katy.

"I grew up in a small town. I was bullied as a child but eventually I started hanging around with a group whose lifestyle impressed me. For the first time I felt accepted. By the age of 16 we were experimenting with drink and drugs and the partying began.

"Unfortunately I started getting into trouble with the local police and was involved in three separate alcohol-related car crashes. Separate to this, a good friend then died in a car accident which totally devastated me.

"On New Year's Eve 1997, a friend was throwing a party. His father was away. There were over 150 guests, and with so much drugs and alcohol going around fights started breaking out. When a stranger came up the stairs and asked us all to leave, my friend hit him. He fell to the ground and I kicked him four times in the head. After that I moved on to another party, not knowing I'd made the worst mistake of my life.

"Throughout the investigation the secret of my crime began to destroy me. I became depressed and introverted. I could well have committed suicide if, after four years, I hadn't broken my silence. My family was devastated.

"Having admitted my guilt, I wanted to apologize face-to-face for what had happened.

"So, within an hour of being arrested, I wrote a letter to Katy and her children, apologizing for what I'd done. I also asked a police officer if I could meet with Katy. I'd read about Katy in the papers but never expected her forgiveness. If I put myself in her shoes, I think I would have hated the person who had done what I'd done to her.

"The big question I still ask myself is, 'Why did you do this?' And I still can't find an answer. Doing time is easy compared to the guilt I'll have to live with for the rest of my life. But with Katy's forgiveness – I hope that perhaps, one day, I'll be able to forgive myself."

Ryan has since been released from prison. He is employed and happily married with one child. Katy has since written the book, *Walking After Midnight: One Woman's Journey Through Murder, Justice, and Forgiveness*.

For further information you can visit Katy's website **www.katyhutchisonpresents.com**.

7

Forgiving Would Be Reconciling

Should there always be reconciliation if there has been forgiveness? Is the one the necessary mechanical consequence of the other? No, not inevitably. It's an additional nuance that we need to understand, for being "obliged to reconcile" which some people dread, should they ever forgive, may represent a serious obstacle on the path to forgiveness.

By implementing forgiveness, I bear the responsibility of healing the wounds of my heart. I make the choice not to cultivate the hatred that might destroy me. That is my responsibility, the part of the path that I can freely walk on my own.

But what about the other person, the one who did me wrong? Has that person become aware of his deeds, his wrongs? Has he really apologized? Has he ever tried to repair, one way or another? Or has he, contrarily, stuck to his lines? Has he still understood nothing, recognized nothing? Wouldn't he be prone to behave in the same way should the opportunity arise again?

To reconcile, we need both sides. I can walk half the path myself. When inner work has been accomplished, to restore peace in my heart, I can reach the point where I can consider reconciliation with the one who has assaulted me. But it still requires him to walk the other half of the path, which means that it requires becoming aware of himself, and willing to repair, to amend, to change. Without that, reconciliation is impossible, or would be a dirty trick, even an act of weakness or unconsciousness. What would it mean to reconcile with someone who hasn't changed one bit, and who is liable to perpetrate the same acts of violence at any time?

So we can understand those who say, "If I am to be matey with someone on the pretense that I've forgiven him, then forgiving is out of the question." Except that this mechanic articulation of the two persons involved is not, by any means, an obligation. Because if we actually need two people to reconcile, we can still implement forgiveness or healing on our own. We can forgive without reconciling. Reconciliation may still occur later (if the other one does his share), as it may also never be possible. In all cases, it's never an obligation that comes with forgiveness, nor is its codicil inescapable. These are two different things, though they are linked, but not integral parts of one another.

> "While we actually need two people to reconcile, we can still implement forgiveness or healing on our own. We can forgive without reconciling."

Sylvie's Testimony

"I was still, at the age of 53, deeply wounded by the decision my mother had made to terminate her pregnancy after I had been conceived. It hadn't worked, I had stayed. But the bitterness of anger, and the spur of fear filled my life. Yet, I was on the path towards my main goal: peace on earth.

"During a *Gift of Forgiveness* weekend, I chose – by chance – to listen to a woman who was telling me about her great sadness and deep guilt at not wanting to greet her daughter in her womb. She was to be born anyway. I was shattered . . . I was hearing my mother's point of view, and I could feel boundless compassion for all women who have no desire for the child they are bearing, 'when the time is not the right time'.

"The next day, when the time came to ask for forgiveness from the people in our circle, my heart re-opened wide when I found myself facing this wonderful woman, and I sobbed tears of joy.

"The re-opening of my heart appeased my mind for several weeks, and . . . how deliciously refreshing it was. Since then, I can tenderly say 'my beloved mother' as if the little confident girl I had never been was re-awakening.

"I am happy about all that, and I am taking this opportunity to express my gratitude."

8
Mistaking the Person
and the Action

L ittle Eric cries: "Tom is nasty!", when his friend refuses to lend him his toy. Reducing a person in this way to one or another of his actions, in particular the most negative ones, has unfortunately far from completely disappeared in adulthood. We just need to see how easy it is for people to call others names – in politics, in the media, at work, everywhere. This only leads to acknowledging that attacks *ad personam* are commonplace. Instead of criticizing such choice, such decision, or such action of a politician, a celebrity or my next-door neighbor, I judge them on the whole, without discrimination.

In the practice of forgiveness, mistaking a person and his actions, may also be a major hindrance. If, after being laid off, I state that "my boss is a dirty bastard", not only do I hide all the other decisions he has made in his firm for years (that cannot all be bad), but I also hide what he is as a father, a husband, a friend and a man, which I totally ignore. My mental representation is not that of a person any more: it's a crude caricature, the lively and grotesque manifestation of a flaw, of a defect that I'm completely obsessed with. The painful and violent emotions that overwhelm me – rightly – have entirely taken the upper hand – wrongly. I am no longer able to be impartial, no longer able to stand back from this individual: my mind and my reflection are disconnected.

To an extreme degree, if the actions involved are particularly malevolent or criminal ones, we may go so far as to demonize their author. At this point, there is no longer a human being before us, but the incarnation of a demon. In excluding the other from the very notion of humanity, by turning him into an alien, into an "other", in the most extreme meaning of the word, it then becomes practically impossible to walk the path to forgiveness.

Conversely, as several testimonies from the *Forgiveness Project* stress, it's in discovering the person as a whole, beyond the action he is blamed with, that it becomes possible to put the gesture back into a more global, less simplistic context – without supporting it either – and possible to maybe understand the ins and outs of it. The action itself will remain what it is, in all its ugliness or horror, but beyond it, an entire person will take shape, in all his humanity, his journey, his lights and his shadows.

An action may be unacceptable, even unforgivable, but does it mean that those who committed it are unforgivable? Isn't there anything in common between them and me? Am I absolutely sure of how I would have acted, had I lived their life, had I been in the same situation? Can't I at least detect within them a part of humanity, of light, to rely on, so that I don't completely demonize them, nor deprive myself of any chance of restoring peace in my heart?

Forgiveness is a virtue, that relies both on the heart and the mind. The heart alone does not always suffice. At times, we need to love humans to understand them. At other times we need to understand them to love them. In order not to be overwhelmed by our emotions, and lose all discernment towards the ones who wronged us, the solution is to broaden our understanding, to step back, to not be limited by appearances, to better make out the intricacies of the causes that led to the event undergone.

> "Forgiveness is a virtue, that relies both on the heart and the mind. The heart alone does not always suffice. At times, we need to love humans to understand them. At other times we need to understand them to love them."

So it's the mind, here, that can help make the distinction between the action and the person who committed it. It can enable us to have a broader view of the situation, to pull us out of the turbulent waters of our emotions to help us rise intellectually, where things take on more depth and more shades.

But beware: it's not, conversely, a question of minimizing the action to clear its author. The idea is, once more, to bear two apparently contradictory attitudes at the same time: being able to discriminate and condemn a hurtful or criminal action, while maintaining a global and balanced 3-D vision (depth included) of the person who committed it. Very "decent people" – as they are sometimes called – can commit dreadful actions. It would obviously be much easier if, on the one hand, there were nasty people who only did horrible things, and on the other hand nice ones who always did good. But we are not in fairy tales, and real life is much more complex and paradoxical than that.

Besides empathy, magnanimity or mercy, forgiveness also appeals to our discernment, our ability to step back, and to the sharpness of our judgement. We need both the heart and the mind.

9
Seeing Only the Personal Dimension of the Action

I n the wake of the previous obstacle, this one draws us further into the possibility of better understanding the painful events we go through, therefore into the means at our disposal to possibly reach forgiveness one day. By using our mind again, we must learn to go beyond the personal dimension of the actions we have been the victims of, to also take into account their collective, symbolic, and transpersonal ramifications. Let's go further into this issue.

In his international best-seller *The Four Agreements*,[6] don Miguel Ruiz says – in the second agreement – "Whatever happens, don't take anything personally." For many people, this command aims at setting us free from the negative opinions of others: no matter what others call me, what they say about me, I will not take it personally. It's a start, but for don Miguel Ruiz, implementing this agreement goes way beyond this first step. He says, "If someone steps into your home and shoots you with a shotgun, don't take it personally." It's hard to believe! How can we not take *that* personally?!

The idea underlying this surprising recommendation is that, in fact, the other doesn't – or the others don't – see me as I really am. On the one hand, as psychology teaches us, we use one another as screens for our mutual projections. So I project the flaws I refuse to see in myself onto others. And the others do the same onto me. It's the old biblical story of the sawdust (in our neighbor's eye) and the plank (in our own eye).

And on the other hand, whether we like it or not, we embody various things in the eyes of others: we are living symbols for them. For instance, in my case, I may represent various things for the per-

---

[6] Don Miguel Ruiz, *The Four Agreements* (Amber-Allen Publishing Inc., 2018).

son speaking to me, depending on his or her personal sensitivity: an intellectual, a Swiss (for the French), a Frenchman (for the Swiss), a Clerc, a tall man (more than 1.80 m), a man, a father, a public figure, an old man (for a teenager), a middle-class man, etc.

This means that, when people attack me verbally or physically, it's not just me – myself – that they are after, but everything I represent for them, in that moment, consciously or unconsciously. *Through me*, it is maybe the hatred they feel for the whole group I involuntarily symbolize that is let out. For example, we all know that when a journalist or a French hostage is killed in some foreign country, the terrorists are actually after *France* through that person. There is nothing *personal* in that. This example clearly shows the non-personal dimension – collective or transpersonal dimension – in such an event. However, it's not as obvious in situations that common people undergo, but it's still there, though more unconsciously, more hidden.

The husband who is humiliated every day by his wife may represent for her, *Man* with a capital "M". And this rekindles within her, unhealed wounds with various men, earlier in her life, starting with her own father. It's the same thing the other way around, with a man who hits his wife, and whose basic violence, through her, aims at a different goal, be it *the* women – or some of them – he has suffered from in the past.

Each individual person we are, represents, despite ourselves, one or many collective ones in the eyes of others: *the* immigrants, *the* bosses, *the* sportsmen or women, *the* rich, *the* teachers, *the* children, *the* unemployed, and so forth.

One evening in the news on television, the newscaster announced a new attack in Israel. A Palestinian had bombed himself in a populated neighborhood. A Jewish mother had just lost her seven-year-old daughter. In a knee-jerk reaction, despite the absolute horror of the situation, this woman expressed herself in front of the cameras, putting the unspeakable personal situation she had just experienced into a wider collective dimension.

"Through this terrorist, and through my daughter," she pointed out, "it's part of the whole tension accumulated between Israel and Palestine that blew out today." Her testimony deeply moved me.

For in stretching our understanding of what happens to us the way this woman was able to do, it's the possible paths to forgiveness that broaden at the same time.

If I limit the violent actions I have undergone to mere interactions between my aggressors and me, the channels through which forgiveness can flow are reduced to a single one: the one linking this person to me. Conversely, if I can perceive behind my aggressor his family, the social background he grew up in, the political, social or religious influences exerted on him, and so forth, and if, at the same time, I'm aware of everything I may represent for him, through my appearance and whatever I belong to, then through him and through myself, there are two groups through which forgiveness may flow in various ways.

Each one of us is like a bamboo: under the unique, visible stem, there is a wide network of invisible, underground roots. We are connected to one another through many links, many relationships. We are rooted in a specific social compost. Therefore, what happens to us hardly ever concerns us only. Of course, we are *personally* affected by what happens to us. But *not taking this personally* means letting things go through us without holding onto them, without keeping them, neither one way nor the other.

The wrong that reaches me aims at further than me, so it's better not to hold it back by *taking* it personally. It's better to let it flow through me just like a lightning conductor allows lightning to discharge through it into the ground so it doesn't retain this phenomenal tension within it.

In a similar way, the way I perceive others doesn't stop at them or how I see them. It goes through the others, to take their roots into account too, the sap of which flows through them. In doing that, I open up tracks in them and especially in myself, and by preserving this opening – where I would be tempted to close and to block out everything when faced with suffering – I will ease, in time, the healing process of forgiveness. On the contrary, if I lock it all up, there is congestion, clotting, coagulation, and nothing flows through me or is alive in me anymore. I durably delay this revival of love that forgiveness may represent.

"The wrong that reaches me aims at further than me, so it's better not to hold it back by taking it personally. It's better to let it flow through me just like a lightning conductor allows lightning to discharge through it into the ground so it doesn't retain this phenomenal tension within it."

Nowadays, we are the sad inheritors of a very materialistic and limited vision of what human nature is, even if the progress made in biology, psychology and physics in the last fifty years have harmed this vision to create a much fuller one that will probably reach the public and educational systems in a few years only. This individualistic and narrow view we have of ourselves, in which we each seem like an isolated and independent entity, deprives us from a wider and fairer understanding of what we really are. As a consequence, it makes the path to forgiveness, that some of us still try to take, oddly more complicated.[7]

In a forest, if you only look at the trunks, you will have the feeling of seeing a multitude of trees that are isolated from one another. However, whether you consider their underground roots, or their branches in the sky, these trees are closely linked: separating them is an illusion. Through them, it's the Sky and the Earth that share their mutual energies in many ways.

This image may be used as a prop to imagine that we too, beneath our apparent separation, our individualism and our isolation, are much more linked to one another than we've been taught we are. Therefore, what affects us, what goes through us, affects much more than just our little person, however painful this may sometimes seem. Becoming aware of this, developing and cultivating it[8] without, for that matter, minimizing or eliminating the pains we experience, may unquestionably give us a much deeper understanding, that will, in turn, open up new paths to a liberating forgiveness.

---

[7] See *The Metaphor of the Two Clouds* on page 137 of this book.

[8] I particularly recommend the works of Rupert Sheldrake, which have brought to light in a fascinating way the unsuspected links that exist not only between human beings, but also in the mineral, plant and animal worlds. His work has been taken up by many disciplines over the last thirty years.

Practical Method #3

Ho'oponopono: The Hawaiian Approach to Forgiveness

Originally, *Ho'oponopono* (which can be translated into "re-establishing balance" or "putting things back into their right place") was a Hawaiian collective practice, led by a healer priest.

In modern times, this method has encountered several successive changes. Morrnah Simeona (a well-known healer in Hawaii) turned it into a tool that we can use alone, individually. She also added to it various notions, drawn from her Christian roots, and from reading Eastern books. Then, Dr Hew Len (Morrnah Simeona's former student and administrator) made it really popular in its present shape, in particular thanks to Joe Vitale's book *Zero Limits*. Later on, Dr Len firmly distanced himself from this book.

This very simple method relies on the following four phrases: *"I'm sorry. Please forgive me. I love you. Thank you."* There are some very close variations like *"Sorry. Forgive me. Thank you. I love you."* This four-fold formula appeals to four qualities.

1. First, responsibility: saying "I'm sorry" is acknowledging our share of responsibility in what happened. Responsibility, not guilt, I would like to stress that.

2. Then, forgiveness: "Please forgive me" in which we can see the act of asking for forgiveness, not that of granting it.

3. Third, love: "I love you", which comes naturally after forgiveness, is the "revival of love" as we have defined it.

4. To conclude, gratitude: "Thank you" is the natural expression of a healed heart. I like to say that if forgiveness is the healing of the heart, gratitude is the song of the heart.

> "If forgiveness is the healing of the heart,
> gratitude is the song of the heart."

According to the founding story of the modern version of *Ho'oponopono* (or its legend, it doesn't really matter), Dr Hew Len managed alone to empty an entire wing of a psychiatric hospital, where criminals were confined, just by using the repetition of this formula, without even meeting these prisoners. Indeed, for Dr Len, each one of us is completely responsible not only for the actions we have committed ourselves, but also for those of others. He writes: "The problem is not external reality, it's inside, and to change it, we have to change ourselves. When we bear responsibility for our life, we are completely responsible for everything we see, we hear, we feel or learn, one way or another, since it's part of our own perception of life."[9]

Faced with the negative actions of others, the *Ho'oponopono* principle consists therefore in working on ourselves, in freeing ourselves from the judgements, the accusations, and the negative emotions

---

[9] At least, those are the words quoted by Joe Vitale in his book *Zero Limits*.

that find echoes in us. The underlying idea is that humanity is fundamentally one: if I change myself, I transform others too. Rather than putting the blame on others, rather than posing as a judge or a victim, I bear my share of responsibility and free myself, cleanse within me whatever echoes the wrongdoings of others. This is a work that might, as in Dr Len's founding story, have an impact on others as well, even if the main use of working on forgiveness – to my mind – is first freeing *oneself* from that very stranglehold of hatred and the poison of resentment.

As far as I am concerned, I have often used, "*I am sorry, I apologize, I love you, Thank you*", just like a mantra, without necessarily feeling the need to support various beliefs that have recovered this practice in the past fifty years. This mantra is as simple as it is powerful. And I have, time and again, been convinced of its effectiveness and its deep power to transform. It's possible, and in fact very likely, that working with this method can have a beneficial effect on others. However, the main thing for me is to first enjoy the therapeutic effect on oneself, for those who practice it. While I am absolutely convinced of our interdependence, and of the positive impact on others of what each of us undertakes to better ourselves, I'm very careful when faced with the possibility – and reality – of drifting towards what is called "magical thought". With it comes the risk of reviving a hidden and insidious childish omnipotence: "I can control everything through my thoughts, my feelings, my intentions. I'm responsible for everything. I can create everything, etc."

Practicing *Ho'oponopono* is undoubtedly efficient, without needing to subscribe to certain beliefs that it didn't support in the first place. As Morrnah Simeona and Dr Len did, each in their own way, you can also take on this beautiful method to suit yourself, adapt it to your own philosophy, and your own beliefs. You do not necessarily have to swap them for any others.

At a time when many Hindu and Tibetan mantras have become popular – that are indeed very beautiful, powerful and effective (like the famous *Om Mani Padme Hum*) – I like to point out that many prayers and formulas in English, stemmed from various old or contemporary traditions, can also have a very deep effect if we repeat them tirelessly, and with awareness! *"I am sorry, please forgive me, I love you, thank you"* or *"Sorry, I apologize, thank you, I love you"* are also very powerful mantras, or at least can be used as such, to the great advantage of those who use them.

10
Wanting to Understand Immediately What You Are Experiencing

As we deal with this tenth obstacle, we're going deeper into what may be happening within us, most of the time unknowingly, when we undergo hardship, injustice or aggression. Understanding these unconscious psychological mechanisms may help us not only to become aware of them, but also to change them so as not to suffer their destructive works.

Let me give you a concrete example to illustrate this. At the age of 57, George was suddenly laid off from his job in an engineering practice in Lausanne where he had been working for thirty years. At the time, as Swiss employment law allowed it, and despite his years of good and faithful service, he was granted no redundancy payment. Cold dismissal!

You can imagine the kind of emotions such an upheaval may cause in a life. He went through everything: anger (towards his bosses and himself), fear (faced with an uncertain future), dejection, deception at not having been at least able to convey his experience to the younger engineer who was going to replace him for half his salary.

To these first two levels – the facts (his dismissal) and the emotions felt – we can add a third one: the intellectual comprehension of the situation, which is the meaning his mind would attempt to give this event. In the grip of his emotions and his knee-jerk reactions, his mind immediately found an explanation *justifying* his feelings: *"My boss is a bastard", "Fate is unrelentingly against me", "Life is unfair", "I'm a victim", "I'm useless"*, and so on. George quickly built what Dr Fred Luskin[10] calls a *"grievance story"*. It's the interpretation

---

[10] Fred Luskin, *Forgive For Good* (HarperOne, revised edition 2003).

we make, when in the grip of a painful situation, that we will tell our relatives, and which we will constantly be turning over, until we end up identifying with it and locking ourselves into. George became the "man who had been laid off from his job at the age of 57, with no redundancy payment". As soon as he met someone for the first time, it took him no longer than fifteen minutes to slip it into the conversation, "You know what? A year (five, ten years . . .) ago, I was laid off . . . etc, etc."

You may be wondering where the problem is.

The problem is that this complaint tale is *one* possible interpretation of what happened to him, *one* possible explanation of the events, but it certainly isn't the only *one*. And, it's not necessarily true: it's most probably partial, biased, and distorted by his emotions.

The other problem is that in *believing* this interpretation made in the spur of the moment, without taking the time to find others, George makes it real *for himself*, and ends up locking himself in a cocoon woven with dark thoughts and bound by his negative emotions. By doing this, he cuts himself off from reality, and closes the door to any possible evolution of the situation.

His emotions end up encysted in his story, forming an emotional and unhealthy abscess. Forgiveness – the healing of that wound – thus becomes all the more difficult to encounter.

In this story, it took George three years to get going again. Three years of depression, anger, hatred, doubt, and despair, before taking the opportunity to set up his own business. This decision thus enabled him to develop personal resources he didn't know he had. He enjoyed his new independent life so much that, a few years later, he told anyone who would listen to him that, "Being fired at the age of 57 was *the best thing* that could have happened to me in my life!" He had completely changed his vision, his understanding and his interpretation of the same situation, the same events.

Is there anyone who hasn't experienced that?

The more you yield to the knee-jerk temptation of understanding a tragic event in the grip of emotions, the more you risk building up simplistic, binary explanations – such as the others are wrong, I am right, I am a victim – and the harder it will then be to dissolve this grievance story, and to heal the emotional cyst it harbours.

So you'll need to walk a long path before reaching forgiveness and peace of heart.

Conversely, if you manage to postpone your immediate interpretation, take the time to cope, let your emotions flow through you and end up wearing them out, neither justifying them nor amplifying them with an elaborate, intellectual explanation and no hindsight; better yet, if you manage to toy with the idea – in accordance with various spiritual teachings – that these painful events may end up having a positive purpose (even if you find this hard to believe while in the grip of your knee-jerk reaction), then everything remains open inside you instead of encysting. So, when your emotions calm down, when the time gone by allows you to step back from the painful event, then one or several less biased, less partial, less conditioned ways of understanding the meaning of what you experienced may emerge. And, at the same time, your chances of reaching forgiveness one day will increase.

The idea, here, as we have already mentioned, is to manage to separate heart and mind. To let the heart experience all the emotions that unexpected, conflictual or violent situations may cause, while deferring our judgement, our intellectual understanding of events, for the time it takes for the level of water to decrease – symbolically speaking – and to start having a clearer vision of things.

In many cases, it's not so much *what happened* that prevents us from implementing forgiveness, but rather how our heart and our mind have dealt with the situation, as Ingrid Betancourt pointed out for herself. It's the grievance story they have unconsciously made up together. It's the emotional cyst that has developed within us, from our lack of awareness of how this inner couple works, secreting feelings and thoughts until we are locked inside of them.

> "In many cases, it's not so much what happened that
> prevents us from implementing forgiveness, but rather how
> our heart and our mind have dealt with the situation,
> as Ingrid Betancourt pointed it out for herself.
> It's the grievance story they have unconsciously
> made up together."

We cannot change the facts: what happened really happened. Period. In the same way, it's hard to change the emotions these facts trigger in us: it's possible, but it takes quite a long path of personal evolution to transform our way of reacting to events. So, the best way we have for freedom and action is on the third level, on the mental or intellectual level: learning how to see the same situation from different angles, looking for possible positive consequences even for what seems the most painful at the time, refusing a unique interpretation, the single tale. It's precisely what is expected of a trained intellect, the fact of keeping a multiplicity of visions without which there is no real freedom of thought. However, it's not when confronted with the most dramatic situations that we can develop it: it's when faced with small everyday humiliations, with the little annoyances of the day, with minor conflicts or ordinary humdrum hitches that we can train "that muscle". You can even have fun – with a good sense of humour – looking at an event from different angles, and getting into the habit of not letting your mind get overwhelmed and enslaved by your emotions.

Training that way – just like others will train in martial arts – may help you acquire amazing self-defence abilities against your own unconscious mechanisms that are often major hindrances not only to forgiveness, but to happiness, a fulfilled life, healthy relationships with ourselves and others.[11]

If the facts (what happened) dictate my emotions, and if my emotions then determine my way of thinking and understanding the situation, where is my freedom? I don't have any! Everything is automatic, mechanical and unconscious. But forgiving is precisely recovering the freedom to love. Gaining this freedom means becoming aware of our own way of functioning, deciding to change that, and regularly implementing other relationships between our heart and our mind, until these new habits get the upper hand over the old ones. It is a path to awareness, action, and emancipation.

---

[11] I have created several tools to work towards that goal in my books *Mettre de l'ordre en soi* (Trédaniel, 2012) and *J'arrête de (me) juger* (Eyrolles, 2014).

Patrick's Testimony

"I attended the *Gift of Forgiveness* workshop in 2012. It was a moment of rare authenticity, followed by a liberating intensity that words alone cannot express. As far as I am concerned, I experienced it as a path at the end of which there was a door, the door to forgiveness. When I reached it, I naturally knocked on it so it would open. And to my amazement, the door opened because I was ready. Understand: it was my heart that was ready, not my mind. For opening the door to forgiveness is like opening the door to your heart that is locked from the inside, having always held its key tight without knowing it.

"The unconscious prisoner of my actions, my thoughts, my words, throughout my whole life, this wonderful tool now makes me aware not only of how locked up and how isolated I am, but also of how every instant of my life has stiffened, and crystallized, instead of letting it flow freely.

"In my personal experience, every time my eyes met those of someone else while asking for forgiveness, the same intense energy – that I would now call a blessing – came to strike us, to cleanse us, to purify us through a continuous flow of tears. I stopped trying to understand, to greet that intense moment of sharing among those attending the workshop, in a quasi-religious silence, in a beauty that connected us to our humanity, that I'm not ready to forget.

"I've become more human thanks to this work. If God sleeps in a stone, wakes up in a plant, enters an animal, and revives as a human being (a Hindu proverb), then this weekend has allowed me to bring part of my humanity to life in making me responsible for letting love or life, from now on, flow consciously. It's a ritual, so the work doesn't stop here. As Jacques Salomé (a famous French psycho-sociologist) puts it, 'What I say belongs to me, what you hear belongs to you, and what you do with it is your responsibility.' I now feel responsible for passing this gift on further now, in my own way."

11
Forgiveness and Arrogance

In this list of obstacles to forgiveness, I believe it's necessary to broach the subject of arrogance, often considered as one of the most important ones. Arrogance can indeed prejudice a real work of forgiveness in three different ways. These, as we will see, entail separate adjustments.

In its most widely spread manifestation as regards forgiveness, arrogance is a posture that consists in being certain of our legitimacy, in looking at others from above, in feeling superior to them, in considering we're entitled to judge them be it mercilessly, never wanting to let go, never conceding. "Forgiving?," says Arrogance in this case, "Never! That person does not deserve it. I will not grant him or her that. It's not that I *can't* (some people would like to forgive but cannot): I don't *want* to. I refuse it. My ego is adamantly and implacably against it."

In the light of what has previously been said, it is ignorance hiding behind the ego. The people who take up this posture don't know that in behaving that way, they're penalizing *themselves* first: they're preventing themselves from healing, loving, and living fully. They may believe they're defending themselves. They use their arrogance as an armour, as a bastion, as a protective distance from their aggressor. Or they may hope to harm the other in refusing forgiveness?

This attitude altogether loses its relevance, its logic, and its obvious pertinence as soon as we understand that it's our *own* healing that is at stake, our own inner peace. Arrogance harms much more the person who demonstrates it than the one it's aimed at. Lack of forgiveness too. When I believe that by locking myself up, by becoming tougher, by refusing forgiveness, by being self-righteous, by transforming myself into an uncompromising judge, I can reach the goals I long for (i.e., justice for my aggressor and recovered peace for myself), I'm in a kind of spiritual blindness.

I believe this first type of arrogance, that stems from ignorance, can be defused by the brand new understanding of what forgiveness is, as shown in these pages.

The second type of pride that can make forgiveness more complicated is subtle, and not as obvious to recognize. It is what I call "forgiveness-arrogance". What I mean here is the posture that consists in pouring out forgiveness onto someone else, from our ivory tower, with a magnanimity that is only condescension. It's a purely mental forgiveness; the heart has nothing to do with it. It may even hide taking power over someone, in a way.

That form of forgiveness is a delusion, an illusion. It neither heals the one granting it, nor the one receiving it.

There can only be true forgiveness in humility. I would even say that humility is certainly one of the main keys to implementing forgiveness. And when we sometimes find it difficult to forgive, it mostly comes from the humble posture we need to adopt. Letting go, giving up our judgements, replacing this inner mental tension that blocks everything with for-give-ness. Once again, "humility" comes from "humus", the soil, like "human". In forgiveness, you will discover the attitude that consists in laying down the heavy burden of judgements and accusations that is crushing you. You're not in your ivory tower anymore, you're at ground-level, on the same level as the others, on equal footing with them. And, once again too, this form of forgiveness, with that kind of humility, does not prevent discernment and appealing to justice and to penalties equal to the seriousness of the actions committed.

So there is a form of arrogance that blocks any kind of forgiveness, but there is another form that *blends* with it, and perverts its nature to the point where there is no therapeutic efficiency and no healing anymore. Under the pretense of fictitious healing, the wound is still there.

> "So there is a form of arrogance that blocks any kind of forgiveness, but there is another form that *blends* with it, and perverts its nature to the point where there is no therapeutic efficiency and no healing anymore."

Finally, there is a third and last type of arrogance, seldom acknowledged as such in fact, which is mainly an obstacle to forgiveness towards *oneself*. This kind of arrogance is hidden behind an attitude of total self-disparagement: "I'm so guilty, so bad, so hopeless, that I don't deserve to be forgiven." Those who breed such feelings and thoughts believe – under the pretext of belittling themselves – they are showing humility in shrivelling up that way. In fact, it's quite the opposite. Behind this self-crushing, there is a proud, self-assured, ruthless and implacable judge. And this judge places himself above everything: above human justice, above life, above God himself! Think about it: isn't it extraordinary pride to believe we are more qualified in judging ourselves than any human, natural or divine authority? Who does that judge think he is? Where does he think he gets the power he exercises over ourselves from?

"Modesty is pride of the weak," said a wise man for whom this falsely humble attitude was the opposite of genuine humility. Pulling out of this feigned posture, and recovering the genuine humility that it takes for forgiveness, requires having a clear eye, and the honesty to acknowledge what's going on within us, and deciding to depose this tyrannical judge.

So there are three different expressions of arrogance, that can hinder, or get in the way of implementing forgiveness. But in the end, there is the same remedy each time: humility. By the way, how can we define this virtue? Maybe, quite simply, as being aware that there is something (or someone) bigger than us: God, life, nature, the great order of things, depending on our individual beliefs. Being humble is knowing that we are not the highest authority entitled to judge others and ourselves. It's knowing how to commit to higher than ourselves. It's by opening up to what goes beyond us that the power cut off by humility can be re-established, and that forgiveness can manifest through us.

The Forgiveness Project
The story of Yulie Cohen (Israel)

I made friends with a Palestinian deportee
and began to see that the so-called enemy
were just people like him.

Yulie Cohen was a 22-year-old El Al stewardess when, in 1978, she was wounded in a terrorist attack in London which left one person dead and many injured. Two years earlier she had been an officer in the Israeli Army at the time of the raid on Entebbe Airport in Uganda. The raid resulted in the deaths of three hostages and several soldiers at the hands of terrorists. Now, over two decades later, she has written to the British Home Office asking for the release of the gunman who wounded her in the El Al attack.

"I wasn't born a pacifist. I was ten years old when the 1967 war began and Israel was being threatened with elimination. I was always going to do my military service to defend my country. I never doubted our righteousness and was eager to prove myself in a man's game.

"But when I was shot at by a Palestinian terrorist that day in London, it didn't occur to me that he was the enemy. I could see that he and I were a small part of a bigger game. My grandma spoke Arabic – how could the Arabs be 'the enemy'.

"Even so, after I graduated from University, I joined the army again, this time as a communications attaché. It was through my journalistic activities that I began to see through the myths to the lies that were being told by my own government. It was the beginning of my doubts about the choices we had made as a nation, and about our continued policies of aggression.

"My parents were strong Zionists, but my brother rejected their stance. As a 17-year-old he could not handle the clash between his family's ideals and the reality of life in Israel, so he took a 180-degree turn and became an orthodox Jew. Significantly, the more they challenged him, the more extreme he became.

"In 1948 Israel had a just war – we needed a homeland for the Jews. In 1967, we had to defend that homeland. In 1973, war was forced on us. But then it started to collapse. In 1978–79 we had peace with Egypt, but we forgot to change the cassette. We carried on as if we were still at war, even though we were not. The truth – the reality – was not being told. Jordan made peace with us. Egypt, Lebanon, Syria – they all wanted to help us sort out the problem with the Palestinians. But no: we had to keep them as our enemies and ourselves as the victims.

"Still, it was not until 1999 that I became really clear in my thinking. I made friends with a Palestinian deportee and began to see that the so-called enemy were just people like him. I started to learn about the Palestinians, and about my own history too; so much information that I lacked, and information that now allowed me to understand.

"And *understanding is the starting point. You can't forgive without understanding.* Young people are easily brainwashed: whether it's to go into the army or to become a terrorist, they are used to settle state interests, not their own, and not mine. I stopped being an agent of the state's story and started to write my own.

"That's when forgiveness began. It started with the man who shot me. I tried to have a dialogue with him, but he didn't want that: he had moved on and wanted to leave his past behind. So I began to lobby for his release and still do until today. I realized that it's not about him – or about us – it's about me.

"We become the victims of ourselves if we don't forgive because the hate is within us, it doesn't belong to the other. It's a process to free yourself from your own suffering.

"I wasn't going to raise my daughters in the way our parents raised us. I could see nothing to live for with that black-and-white approach that continues to lead people to war. In that way, a terrorist is exactly the same as a soldier: they are both brainwashed. When you see reality in a complex way it's more difficult, but more interesting and rich.

"Once I had felt forgiveness for my attacker, I saw that I also had to forgive my parents for the deceptions they had allowed and were continuing to uphold. Some of my family followed my example, but some didn't. My brother no longer meets me or speaks to me.

"There are moments when I am very lonely, but, for the first time in my life, I am being loyal to myself. For me that is the most important part of it."

Yulie has produced three documentaries, *Lev Haaretz* (2001), *My Terrorist* (2002), and *My Land Zion* (2005).

You can find more information about Yulie and her documentaries on her website: **https://yuliecohen.wixsite.com**.

12
Asking for Forgiveness Would Induce Feeling Guilty

I have already had the opportunity to briefly discuss this obstacle in my book *The Gift of Forgiveness*,[12] but I will bring it up again here, as I will for the following obstacle. Yes, for many of us, the very notion of forgiveness conveys guilt. This is what approaches such as the *Gift of Forgiveness*, *Ho'oponopono*, or some religions' traditions that stress the art of *asking for forgiveness*, more than that of forgiving, may give rise to at first.

We can actually ask for forgiveness being burdened by guilt. We can use it not as a way to become more responsible, to heal our wounds, and to free ourselves, but as a way to belittle ourselves, to shrivel up, to find ourselves hopeless or pathetic, and to give others or our inner judge all power over us. It's true that we can wallow in guilt in a completely morbid and unproductive way.

Many of us have more or less learned how to practice forgiveness this way. When we require a child to ask for forgiveness, in a very accusing and judgmental voice, we may be granted a whispered "Sorry", with a downward glance. But, on the one hand we create, in the mind of the child, an unhealthy link between forgiveness and feeling guilty, and on the other hand we teach the child to forcibly express an artificial request for forgiveness which does not stem from the heart, and is not the result of a natural and fair outburst.

Those who have experienced that in childhood may, once adults, tend to completely reject the very notion of forgiveness. To say it again: it would be throwing out the baby with the bathwater (a rather charming expression by the way . . .). It's not because we can draw a link between a pathologically guilt-inducing behaviour and asking for forgiveness that it should *necessarily* be done that way.

---

[12] Olivier Clerc, *The Gift of Forgiveness* (Findhorn Press, 2010).

In the perspective of *Ho'oponopono* or the *Gift of Forgiveness*, the requests for forgiveness that are expressed do not convey guilt, but a feeling of responsibility. They don't belittle those who express them, but rather free them, and help them to grow. By asking for forgiveness, I stop hating, I stop demonizing those who hurt me, I stop using what they said or did at one time or another as a pretext to indefinitely feed my present with a resentment that is destroying me. So I can recover my share of responsibility without, for that matter, denying that of others. I can also recover my own power, and in particular that of healing.

- If I'm the one who has done wrong, I can ask for forgiveness without wallowing in guilt, to concentrate my energy onto repairing what can be repaired, and changing those aspects of my behavior that must be changed. Guilt brings nothing to no-one. It might even risk feeding the ego of whoever needs to take revenge against, and ascendency over, the one who wronged them. Sadly, satisfying.

- If it's someone who has wronged me, and I have gathered lasting resentment or hatred against that person, I can ask that person for forgiveness for having unconsciously used his or her actions and gestures to justify my inner state and make it last. This can, here too, be without guilt: by taking responsibility, by reclaiming power over my inner state, my feelings and my emotions.

You must have noticed, going through the many obstacles to forgiveness, how often it's automatically mistaken with other behaviours or practices when it shouldn't be. Actually, it has to be clearly disconnected from them. A fair practice of forgiveness requires us having a lot of discernment, some reprogramming, and, if needed, unlearning the way we've been imitating until then. How to practice it requires relearning in a more enlightened and balanced way.

Experiencing a workshop or a forgiveness ceremony, based on this new approach, enables acquiring from the inside, from having lived it, and through personal experience, the very steps of which I am detailing here. Basically it's a lot less difficult than it seems.

I'm pointing this out so that you are not under the – groundless – impression that relearning forgiveness is something that takes time and is tedious to undertake. Thousands of people who have taken this path are here to testify the opposite.

"It's not because we can draw a link between a pathologically guilt-inducing behaviour and asking for forgiveness that it should necessarily be done that way."

13
Asking for Forgiveness Would Be Humiliating

This obstacle is closely linked to the previous one. This time, it comes from confusing humiliation and humility. Yes it is humiliating to be forced, from the outside, to ask for forgiveness – in particular as a child – without this request being prompted by a genuine personal awareness, or a natural impulse. In this case, asking for forgiveness boils down to saying publicly: "I'm hopeless, I'm useless, I'm worthless, I'm detestable", etc. To my mind, it's a phony and degrading request for forgiveness that, by the way, fools no-one: the one receiving this conventional request does not believe in it and hardly feels satisfaction, while the one expressing it is far from being always sincere since it's often only being submitted to the requests of adults. Appearances are kept up, but a pseudo-forgiveness doesn't bring the healing that comes with a genuine request.

This forgiveness-humiliation from childhood may distort the understanding we will retain of this process as an adult. It is however possible to free ourselves from that for the benefit of a true attitude of humility, mentioned several times already. What's the difference? I no longer ask for forgiveness because I am forced to, while humbling myself, crumbling before others, in the grip of fright or constraint. I ask for forgiveness because I feel like doing it in my heart, because I understand its meaning and its real goal, because I want to free myself from hatred, from the toxic link of resentment, because I want to heal and recover my inner freedom.

Both attitudes are totally opposed from all viewpoints: in what drives them, as well as in the effects produced; within us, as well as in the others. Humiliation crushes, belittles, and shrivels. Humility frees, helps us grow, and elevates. The first is imposed from the outside. The second can only come from the inside, from our individual growing awareness.

The most genuine forgiveness can only come from the heart, but the heart obeys neither our will nor our reason. Pascal said of the heart that it had its reasons "that reason knew not". We cannot force anyone to sincerely implement forgiveness. Yes, we can humiliate someone, but it's impossible to impose sincere humility. It can only come from within. So, wherever there is humiliation, there is no genuine forgiveness. Only humility enables sincere and true forgiveness.

"Humiliation crushes, belittles, and shrivels. Humility frees, helps us grow, and elevates."

Practical Method #4

The Gift of Forgiveness: Four Progressive Requests for Forgiveness

The approach don Miguel Ruiz passed on to me, was the subject of my book *The Gift of Forgiveness* (already mentioned above), translated into eight languages, and of workshops carried out in about fifteen countries. It's based on a reversal of the normal process of forgiveness. The idea is to learn how to *ask for forgiveness* rather than forgive. This reversal may initially be surprising, seem paradoxical or absurd: why should I ask for forgiveness, especially if I'm the one suffering, the one wounded? Shouldn't it be up to the one who hurt me to say "sorry", to ask for forgiveness, to repair? And shouldn't I be the one to forgive? . . .

The *Gift of Forgiveness* aims at making me free, reclaiming my power and my responsibility. But, if I spend months and years waiting for the other to make the first step, to heal my wounds at last, it may take a long time, it may even take forever (if the other person is dead for example). Healing my heart, in fact, only depends on *me*. When I ask for forgiveness in the ways stated below, I let the others bear the entire responsibility of what they have said or done to me: I ask for forgiveness for the way I used what I underwent, days, months or years ago, for my own behaviours that have never ceased, updating these old wounds, reopening them, and preventing them from healing. Of course it's the other who wounded me first, but since then, I – through ignorance, clumsiness or unawareness – have not ceased rekindling it, or even making it worse.

You will find here, in a shortened version, the four steps of this very simple, short and yet very powerful process.

1. **Ask for Forgiveness from Others.** If I'm alone, I visualize the people with whom I feel emotional knots, and I ask them for forgiveness (for those who hurt me, forgiveness for having used what they did, as a pretext for keeping my heart locked and kindling my resentment and hatred). If I'm in a *Circle of Forgiveness*, these requests for forgiveness can be made between the people attending, through whom these requests will touch those they are intended for, both ways. It's the whole transpersonal power of this ritual that comes into play there, as a group.

2. **Ask my Scapegoats for Forgiveness.** The idea here is to stop demonizing entire groups of people (for example the rich, bosses, polluters, terrorists, members of a certain political party, followers of a certain religion, citizens of a certain country, etc.). We have to take control of our heart again, not let it secrete negative emotions towards anyone, on the basis of prejudice and bias. It's choosing to love, to be a channel for love rather than letting the darkest and most toxic emotions and feelings run though us (therefore poisoning us too) before directing them towards others.

3. **Ask for Forgiveness from "Higher than Myself".** Depending on the philosophy and beliefs of each one of us, this may mean asking for forgiveness from God, from Life or Love with a capital "L", from Earth, Nature, Destiny, Lords of the Karma . . . Who do you blame when life forces hardships onto you? Whom do you reproach the hard blows of your life with? This step allows us to stop using the highest, most beautiful, and most sacred as an additional pretext to brood in our heart. It's an additional projection that we give up, another self-power reclaimed.

4. **Ask Myself for Forgiveness.** This is the last of the four steps, implementing forgiveness for myself. I ask myself for forgiveness, for all the times when I judge myself, when I blame myself, and when I punish myself, for all the times when I'm split up,

in inner conflict, rejecting parts of myself. I make peace within myself, I reconcile with myself, I bring unity within my heart. Depending on our individual beliefs, we can imagine ourselves in the guise of the child we once were, as symbols of innocence and purity, or in the shape of a divine spark, of the spirit that lives within us. And rather than seeking forgiveness from ourselves, we may humbly ask for forgiveness, completely letting go all accusations and grievances we have, in vain, cultivated against ourselves.

As a group in a *Circle of Forgiveness* – with the preliminary exercises – it only takes two or three hours. Alone at home, the process described above can be done in as little as ten or twenty minutes. And it's always like showering the heart, letting all that was crystallizing within us, such as negative or toxic feelings or emotions, flow out.

For more information check the following website:
giftofforgiveness.olivierclerc.com

14

Forgiveness Would Be
a Sign of Weakness

This is a relatively widespread idea, that the fans of the NCIS (special investigations) series will have probably heard of: "Never say you're sorry," special agent Gibbs says once one of his agents – and especially the men among them – has the misfortune of excusing himself. For those who believe in this, asking for forgiveness, or apologizing – that is, acknowledging our mistakes, wanting to repair them – is necessarily admitting our weakness, lowering our guard, inviting reprisal or attacks from the other.

For me this position is the wrong one for two reasons.

First because it gives the impression that the people who never apologize, never ask for forgiveness for their mistakes, are strong. But what kind of strength are we really dealing with here? The strength of denial, of the resistance of the ego, of a merely personal strength that builds on conflict and division. This kind of strength, one that is expended on a daily basis by people who deny responsibility, draws on their own resources: in the end, it weakens them, stiffens them, cuts them off from life. This strength ends up being an illusion, and seems like acknowledging some hidden weakness: "I cannot let go," says that kind of person, "I'm a control-freak, I need to defend myself and protect myself at all costs. I'm in a permanent battle, be it against life itself."

Second, what about the so-called weakness of those who are ready to acknowledge their wrongs, ask for forgiveness, and try to repair? It's the weakness of those who are ready to lay down their too heavy armour, so they can be lighter, more supple, quick and mobile. Take a cockroach: it resists ten times earth's gravitation while humans faint at two or three Gs. But turn this cockroach onto its back, and everything that makes its strength – its shell – keeps it from straightening up alone, and it's doomed to die.

There are apparent forces that can hide fearsome weaknesses, and apparent weaknesses that are really great strengths. Acknowledging our wrongs, knowing how to ask for forgiveness, is freeing ourselves from the crushing burden of judgement, denial, or even hatred. It means becoming lighter. It means getting back into the flow of life and being carried again by it.

John used to say about Christ, "He must increase, but I must decrease." This sentence symbolically means: "The spirit must become greater within me while my ego becomes less." True strength does not lie within the ego, our little limited personality. It's in the spark of life, in the Self that inhabits us. This is the strength that Gandhi, for example, showed, despite being small and lean. A strength that ended up making a whole empire yield, because it was not a personal strength, stemming from the claims or the resistances of his ego.

> "There are apparent forces that can hide fearsome weaknesses, and apparent weaknesses that really are great strengths. Acknowledging our wrongs, knowing how to ask for forgiveness, is freeing ourselves from the crushing burden of judgement, denial, or even hatred."

In reality, unlike appearances, daring to ask for forgiveness requires great inner strength, trusting life, a form of letting go to something higher than oneself. Therefore, it's not necessary to reinforce the defences and ramparts of our ego, to justify ourselves, to protect ourselves, to control everything, to never give in.

It is perhaps because it requires a lot of courage and strength that are not those of the ego, that forgiveness sometimes seems so difficult to implement. Those who dare do it, are freed and strengthened by that experience when they come out of it, not weakened nor diminished.

The Forgiveness Project
The Story of Ginn Fourie and Letlapa Mphahlele (South Africa)

In 1993, Lyndi Fourie was killed in the Heidelberg Tavern Massacre in Cape Town, aged 23. Nine years later, her mother, Ginn Fourie, heard a radio interview with the man who had ordered the attack. Letlapa Mphahlele, the former Director of Operations of the Azanian People's Liberation Army (APLA), the military wing of the Pan African Congress (PAC), was in Cape Town to promote his biography, *Child of the Soil*.

Ginn Fourie

"On the evening of 30 December 1993, a hail of AK-47 gunfire ended our daughter's life and dreams. Lyndi had no time to debate why the PAC wanted white people to suffer as black people had suffered under apartheid, even though she had often wept at the many injustices that black people had endured.

"As parents, we struggled to come to terms with our loss. It was a time of deep agony for me, my husband and our son, Anthony. At the funeral my eldest brother, who conducted the service, recommended that the most appropriate Christian response to violence is to absorb it, just as Lyndi's soft body had done on that fateful day.

"Within a week of the Heidelberg Massacre three young men were detained, and in November 1994 they stood trial. I sat in the Supreme Court in Cape Town, looking at them in the dock: Humphrey Gqomfa, Vuyisile Madasi and Zola Mabala. As I did so, I was confronted by my own feelings of anger and sadness, but somehow I could engender no hate. During the trial I sent a message to them via the interpreter which said, 'If they are guilty or feel guilty, I forgive them.'

"However, I also depended on the law to avenge my loss, and I was relieved when all three were convicted of murder and sent to prison for an average of 25 years each. The Judge described them as puppets: puppets who had carried out a violent crime which had been orchestrated by more cunning and intelligent people than themselves.

"Many could not countenance my forgiveness for Lyndi's killers, but as a Christian I cherished the memory of Christ forgiving his murderers. Since then I have come to understand forgiveness as a process which involves the principled decision to give up your justifiable right to revenge. Because to accept violation is a devaluation of the self.

"At the Truth and Reconciliation Commission hearing in October 1997, I learnt that Lyndi's killers were likely to be granted amnesty, and I did not oppose this. At the conclusion of the hearings the three young men asked to speak to me. They thanked me and said that they would take my message of forgiveness and hope to their communities and to their graves, whether they received amnesty or not.

"Then, in October 2002, I turned on my car radio and heard an interview with Letlapa Mphahlele – the man who had masterminded the Heidelberg massacre. I knew he had been dodging the public prosecutor and had not applied for amnesty, and so with a sense of anger and righteous indignation I took myself down to his book launch.

"During the event I stood up and asked him whether he was trivializing the TRC process by not taking part in it. To my surprise, he responded in a very positive way. He said he could understand why people might think this, but that in his view the TRC had trivialized the fact that APLA were fighting a just war. And why, he asked, while his soldiers were being held in prison, had the apartheid defence forces been spared? I hadn't thought of it like this before, and I welled up with tears. Then Letlapa came straight from the podium to where I was sitting and said, 'I'll do anything if you'll meet with me this week.' In that moment I saw remorse in his eyes. It would have been so much easier if he had been a monster with horns and a tail.

"People said he was unapologetic, but I soon discovered that for Letlapa saying 'sorry' is too easy. He wants to build bridges between our communities to bring conciliation. That October he invited me to his homecoming ceremony and asked me to make a speech. It was here that I was able to apologize to his people for the shame and humiliation which my ancestors had brought on them through slavery, colonialism and apartheid.

"Letlapa's name means 'man of stone' and I feel that he has been weathered by a formidable struggle to become a 'child of this soil'. I too am a child of this soil. I know his comrades' bullets killed my daughter, and that terrible pain will always be with me. But I have forgiven the man who gave the command. I feel his humanity."

Letlapa Mphahlele

"I am an atheist but I believe absolutely in reconciliation, meeting soul to soul, person to person. As human beings, we have to face each other and mend relationships. Getting to know Ginn has been a profound and humbling experience for me. From our first meeting in 2002, Ginn understood me. While others couldn't understand why these terrorists were still unapologetic, Ginn said that she detected remorse in me. By this time all the charges against me had been withdrawn, but still I felt nothing inside. It was only when people extended gifts of forgiveness that the roots of my heart were shaken, and something was restored inside me.

"Since meeting Ginn, I've had to face the fact that people were killed because of my orders. I've also had to acknowledge that the people we fought and harmed and caused to grieve were never our direct enemies. I believed that terror had to be answered with terror, and I authorized high-profile massacres on white civilians in the same way that our oppressors had done to us. At the time it seemed the only valid response. But where would it have ended? If my enemies had been cannibals, would I have eaten white flesh? If my enemies had raped black women, would I have raped white women?

"I have changed since that time and I no longer believe you should meet violence with violence. I now think you can deal with oppression in a more creative way. I believe what Ginn says, that even if violence comes your way, you should 'absorb it'. And that is not the coward's way; it is extremely difficult to do.

"My mission now is to reach out to those who survived, because by meeting together we are able to restore each other's humanity. When Ginn attended my homecoming, she delivered the most moving speech of the day. She stood up and asked for forgiveness on behalf of her ancestors. She also got the loudest applause – louder than I got after nearly two decades in exile.

"Some people have decided not to forgive me for what I have done, and I understand that. It's not easy to forgive, but to those who have forgiven I believe that this is how we start to rebuild our communities. This is an intense human mission. People sometimes ask me if I have also killed people myself, with my own hands. When I am asked this, I never answer. Not because I am afraid of speaking the truth, but because I believe that every foot soldier who killed at my command is less guilty than me, because I authorized the targets. I exonerate those who pulled the trigger. It is I who should shoulder the blame."

Since then both Ginn and Letlapa have been working to further conciliation in South Africa through the Lyndi Fourie Foundation. Ginn and Letlapa also feature in the documentary *Beyond Forgiving*.

The South African Truth and Reconciliation Commission was set up by the Government of National Unity to help deal with what happened under apartheid.

"Vulnerable feelings, when expressed to other people, have the potential to establish lasting bonds."

15
Wanting to Do Things
Too Quickly

We are now reaching the last of the fifteen obstacles to forgiveness. I've often encountered it in the workshops I lead. Because of their religious education, as soon as something painful, violent or traumatizing happens to them, some of them say to themselves: "I must forgive." This obligation, this duty to forgive, is imposed on them by the religious teachings they received, or rather by the understanding they now have of them. Of course, the Bible for example, commands us to forgive "even our enemies", and there are similar injunctions in various other religious or spiritual traditions. But does it mean that these recommendations should be turned into instruments of self-torture? Where is it written that we have to forgive here and now, without waiting . . . ?

We've just seen how our heart doesn't obey our will. No matter how much we want to forgive, if our heart refuses to, we will not manage to. How can we forgive then? How can we submit our own will to a religious command hoping our heart will yield to it?

What prompts this obligation to forgive in those who force themselves to do it? What a shambles! This can naturally kindle a lot of guilt: "I should forgive, but I can't, so I'm not a good Christian [or any other denomination]. I'm not enlightened or spiritual enough." It can also make us repress our emotions, including the most painful ones, as well as our judgements. Repressing them in this way will durably encyst them, preventing any kind of healing. That person will end up in denial, feigning a state that is not really his or hers.

It all stinks, if I'm allowed this expression! It has nothing to do with genuine forgiveness. It's only clumsiness or falseness.

In fact, forgiveness is like a fruit ripening, at its own rhythm, on the branch. We can ease its ripening, but certainly not skip its steps.

The key word here may be steps. Everyone today has heard about the five steps of mourning described by Dr Elisabeth Kübler-Ross: denial, anger, bargaining, depression, and acceptance. In the same way, forgiveness may also involve various steps that may be different from one person to another, depending on what they've had to go through, their beliefs and disposition.

For some, the first step is often accepting and expressing the emotions caused by the painful event instead of repressing or denying them. In his Radical Forgiveness workshops, Colin Tipping (see p. 76) sometimes uses a tennis racket and cushions to enable the people attending to vent, at last, all the anger repressed that prevents them from genuinely taking the path to forgiveness. We can compare an emotion to a wave: if it's small, it will only take a few meters to ebb on the beach; if it's big, it will take a much bigger distance, and if it's an emotional tsunami, it will require a much longer ebbing beach.

Denying an emotion means erecting a barrier in front of it, even if there is the risk of seeing it explode one day. Locking oneself up in a grievance story is letting our mental winds blow violently onto this wave until it doubles or triples in volume. Between denial and amplification, we should ideally let this wave run through us at its own rhythm. Once the threshold is crossed, the next door might already be the one to forgiveness.

I recall a woman attending one of my workshops who wanted to forgive her boss, who was harassing her every day at work! Do you remember the analogy with physical wounds: after being stabbed, how can a wound heal if the attack continues? It's impossible! You must first escape, find security, then find someone to take care of you. It's the same thing for wounds of the heart: you cannot heal those wounds – implement forgiveness – if you continue to be submitted to moral harassment on an everyday basis. So, in the case of that woman, the first step I suggested was to escape, one way or another, from the destructive influence of that boss of hers who had a long-established pervert behaviour (which we generally refer to as being a "narcissistic pervert"). Once safe, it would be high time for her to contemplate working on forgiveness. But not before. In fact, I was happy to see her again two years after that, transformed, and altogether free from her boss's tyranny, and from any kind of hatred or resentment towards him.

What we should keep in mind through this is that we cannot do things too quickly, even in the name of the best religious commandments. "There's a time for everything under the heavens," says the Ecclesiastes. A time to accept what one has undergone. A time to greet our emotions. A time to forgive. A time, if needed, to press charges and ask for repair. These times are not the same for each one of us. Making a rule of them would undoubtedly be a mistake. I feel it's better to learn how to listen to ourselves and to respect ourselves, rather than follow the order of some protocol supposed to be right for everybody, everywhere.

> 'There's a time for everything under the heavens,' says the
> Ecclesiastes. A time to accept what one has undergone.
> A time to greet our emotions. A time to forgive. A time, if
> needed, to press charges and ask for repair.

Forgiveness is not a duty: it's a mercy that we open up to greet within us, when we are ready for it.

The New Territory of Forgiveness

Having now reached the end of this overview of the main obstacles to forgiveness, the land recovering this notion appears much more clearly defined than before, where it encroached upon other notions it should be distinguished and separated from. This very territory – the space for forgiveness – may be much more reduced than before. It does not recover these other plots of land that we call "compulsory reconciliation", "condoning", "religion", "guilt", "humiliation", etc. But in limiting it this way, it mostly becomes much more precise, there is less chance of getting lost. So it's also easier to pace up and down (to implement) without getting lost.

Thanks to the definitions and explanations of the first two chapters, shall we now be able to answer the question raised by the title of this book?

Conclusion
Can Everything Be Forgiven?

W̶e are now back to the initial premise of this book: "Can we heal the wounds of the heart, can everything be forgiven?"

Based on how we redefined forgiveness throughout these pages, and on how we more closely circumscribed its meaning, new light has been shed onto this question, as you've probably been able to glimpse it yourself.

Usually, when we ask ourselves this inevitable question, our centre of gravity is placed on the *others* and not on ourselves: "Can I grant them forgiveness? Do they deserve it? Does the seriousness of their action allow them this gift? Or not?"

But, now we know that implementing forgiveness is first and foremost a gift to *ourselves*. The goal, to say it again, is to free ourselves from the stranglehold of hatred, to dress our wounds, to heal our heart. As a consequence, our centre of gravity is no longer on others, but on ourselves. So the question must actually be reformulated. Instead of asking ourselves: "Can I forgive everything?" (implying: *the others*), we really should wonder "Can I heal myself?" "Whatever wounds my heart has suffered, can I cure them, can I heal them?"

This is quite a reversal of posture!

Our priority is not to find out what forgiveness can bring our aggressor, but what it can bring *us*. We refocus on our own longing for integrity, unity, healing.

Parallel to that, as we've also seen it, granting our own heart this balm of forgiveness does not keep us from also appealing to our mind, our judgement, and using our common sense and intelligence to choose the right attitude when faced with our aggressors, depending on the seriousness of their actions, and on how aware they've become:

- to reconcile?

- to sever all relationships?

- or to go right ahead and bring charge?

"Can I heal my heart however serious the wounds suffered?" That is the real question to ask now that we are reaching the end of our investigation. So it's not an answer to the initial question that the previous chapters have brought us, but a reformulation of that original question since it stemmed from a false understanding of forgiveness as it prevails today. It is only by going deeper into what forgiveness really is – as this famous and clumsy question invited us to do, a question we have all asked ourselves at one point or another – that we can change our point of view, and end up reaching this new way of questioning forgiveness:

"Can I heal the wounds of my heart, however serious the wounds suffered?"

In light of the hundreds of testimonies gathered over the years by the *Forgiveness Project*, and of those I received myself from the people attending workshops and forgiveness circles, the answer is thrice "*YES*":

- Yes, I can heal my heart.

- Yes, I can cure.

- Yes, I can pull out of the vicious circle of hatred, and the stranglehold of resentment.

But don't forget, this kind of forgiveness does not necessarily mean excusing the others, nor does it mean condoning their actions. It doesn't mean either being weak, cowardly, or lenient, bordering on injustice or stupidity. We can implement forgiveness and remain strong. We can free our heart and remain mentally lucid, while acting in a fair way. The love that rekindles forgiveness is a strong and brave love with, on top of it, the wisdom of an enlightened mind, not drowned in emotions.

Can Everything Be Forgiven?

*"We can implement forgiveness and remain strong.
We can free our heart and remain mentally lucid,
while acting in a fair way."*

The initial question, *Can everything be forgiven?* can be deluding. It directs our reflections in the wrong way, because it's in itself the fruit of all the projections and confusion that normally surround the issue of forgiveness. When we change our understanding of forgiveness – and I really hope this book will help you do so – this question becomes irrelevant and disappears. At the same time, without this initial question, we might not have taken the time to deepen this subject until bringing to the surface something that is more genuine and more right.

Two other questions can now replace it:

- What can I do for *myself*? Can forgiveness help me find the peace of heart I long for?

- What's right to do for the *other* who did me wrong? Once my heart is in peace, what do common sense and discernment tell me to do?

With these two questions, I can make the difference between what's happening in my heart and in my mind on the one hand, and on the other hand what I undertake for myself and how I react towards my aggressor. This double distinction underlines the importance of discernment in a genuine practice of forgiveness, as described here many times.

So, going deeper into what forgiveness really is, and how to implement it, is a great message of hope. Yes, it's possible to heal our heart, whatever was undergone. But beware: *possible* does not necessarily mean easy and quick. However, the very existence of this possibility is already a great encouragement within us. By comparison, I know it's *possible* to climb Mount Everest, many highly trained mountaineers have done it. But would I be able to do it today? Not necessarily. However, I know that I can train myself, that I can progressively acquire the strength and condition that are necessary to make this effort that may exceed, for the moment, my physical capacities. If I don't manage to do it immediately, I may be able to in a few weeks, or a few months.

If tomorrow something terrible happened to me, Olivier Clerc, would I be able to implement forgiveness straight away? Maybe not. It would be pretentious for me to be sure of that. My only conviction is that there is a path, and that even if it takes time, even if this path entails various successive steps, it would most probably be possible to take the time needed, at my own pace, as so many others have done.

This is why the testimonies and stories scattered in this book are so inspiring and encouraging. And I'm sure you noticed that they don't come from prophets or heroes, but from people like you and me. Faced with the unspeakable, they have managed to walk that path, each at their own pace, and in their own way. This makes them examples for all of us. They open the way. They uncover possibilities that each of us may try, in turn, to manifest.

Humanity nowadays is sick at heart, on a global scale. From the first to the last page of a newspaper, all we read about is problematic relationships, misunderstandings, conflicts, various forms of aggressions, violence, and war. Behind the apparent diversity of the subjects raised – economy, politics, ecology, health and education, and so on – all we find is human beings faced with other human beings, who don't manage to establish constructive and harmonious relationships, and who cannot manage, in an intelligent way, their disagreements and conflicts. And our modern world is dying of that.

To my mind, forgiveness is not an option, and even less a luxury. It's the unavoidable transition to a better world that many of us long for. There will only be a really new or better world with a new or better heart, one that is healed, freed from its old wounds and sufferings, that stain and distort our relationships with ourselves and with others.

> "To my mind, forgiveness is not an option, and even less a luxury. It's the unavoidable transition to a better world that many of us long for."

Any person who has *experienced* forgiveness knows what I mean. Don't trust my words, check them for yourself. Find the means that speaks to you, the method that inspires you, and then experience this liberation, this healing of the heart. It will change your life forever . . . as my experience in Mexico definitely did mine in 1999.

Have a great healing and I hope it all goes well for you!

The Metaphor of the Two Clouds

As shown throughout this book; the ease or difficulty we feel in implementing forgiveness is closely linked to the *understanding* we have of things: not only of forgiveness itself, but also of what a human being is in all his dimensions, what is really at stake when interacting with one another, and beyond that, what our five senses receive from all that.

For years, in my workshops, I have been using a metaphor of my own invention to illustrate this transpersonal vision of the human being that enlarges and considerably changes our way of understanding things and, as a consequence, how we can act. It relies on various researches and leading-edge works in the fields of biology, physics, psychology and psychotherapy, in particular those of the British biologist Rupert Sheldrake, and those of the American psychiatrist of Czech origin, Dr Stanislav Grof. It offers a transpersonal vision of violence, love and forgiveness.

What does this metaphor say?

The First Cloud

Let's imagine an individual: you, me, anyone. Throughout the day, that person harbours thoughts and experiences, and a wide range of emotions and feelings. And let's imagine that, at certain times, this character is suddenly overcome by a desire for murder: he (for example) cannot stand his boss, his neighbour, his wife, or his mother-in-law, like in a famous cartoon by Tex Avery (entirely grounded on hatred for mothers-in-law!). He feels like taking a shotgun, and getting rid of her. But, being well-behaved, with morals and human values, and knowing how to control himself, he does not turn his dark thoughts and negative feelings into actions. He controls himself.

What do these thoughts and feelings, that have not materialized in his own life, eventually become?

If we stick to what the materialistic vision of things says, the one we were brought up in, what I think remains exclusively in my head, what I feel is only in my heart, and it does not leave it. Some would even say it's a purely chemical process, that is limited to my own person. In the best of cases, psychosomatic medicine acknowledges that these thoughts and feelings may have a harmful influence on the person who cultivates them, and make that person sick. But that's the end of it. Period.

This belief – because that's what it is – is widely refuted by all kinds of experiences made in the past decades. Indeed, they show that our thoughts and feelings are energies, that they spread way beyond our little person, maybe as would waves that interact from a great distance with our computers, our cell-phones, our tablets, our GPSs and other gadgets we all use now.[13] So, when a group of people pray from a distance for sick people in a specific ward in a hospital, these sick people show a higher rate of recovery than those in the ward having no-one to pray for them. These sick people seem therefore to have benefitted unknowingly from the positive energy sent out to them.

Which means that the thoughts and murderous feelings of our fictional character will not remain within the boundaries of his heart or cranium. They will originate and radiate around him. By similarity, they will join other thoughts and feelings with the same vibration, sent out by the whole society, in other words by all of us, you and me, each time we are caught in all kinds of violent desires, that we refrain from

---

[13] Without knowing it, scientists often rediscover processes that already exist in nature, in other forms, mostly more elaborate ones. Our many electronic devices that send out and receive all kinds of invisible and inaudible waves most certainly draw their inspiration from living beings that also tap imperceptible energies (the soul, the mind) and then manifest them through the specific instrument of their bodies.

translating into actions. This can be illustrated by saying that all these darkest feelings and thoughts rise to form a cloud of negativity above our heads.

When a person, then ten people, a thousand people, a hundred thousand people, regularly feed on such feelings and thoughts, a huge, black cloud forms, with the accumulation of an incredible load of violence.

Have you ever seen a cloud forming?

I doubt it. At one point, there it is, in the sky, but we haven't

seen the trillions of drops of water that it is composed of, evaporating from seas, lakes or forests. And can we see its dangerous electromagnetic charge building up? Not at all. Until . . .

Until suddenly a tree, a steeple or a person is struck by lightning and discharges it into the ground. Similarly, in this metaphor, this load of negative intentions suddenly collapses onto a person who *will* act, and concretely express this violence, bringing it to light for everyone as it has become murderous. This person will in actual fact kill his/her boss, husband or wife, or neighbor. That person discharges the energy contained in the cloud.

The second character of my drawing is what we sometimes call the "weak link". It may be someone who has never read a single self-help book, who has never enrolled in a NVC workshop, who has not read the *Four Agreements*, someone who grew up in a particularly unfavourable environment, or who is merely more *receptive* than the average person.

And that's when everybody points at the culprit with horror: "Have you seen what he did? He/She's a monster!" That person, and that person alone, is submitted to public condemnation. From the drawing I sketched above, there only remains the last fourth of it, in the bottom right hand corner,

where lightning struck, the only visible, tangible, obvious and evident part.

Depending on how serious the action is, and depending on the country in which it occurred, the person is arrested, imprisoned, judged, and maybe also executed. But do these measures really take into account the full cycle of violence, its genesis . . . or do they only look at its visible symptom, its concrete outward expression?

I want to point out immediately that this transpersonal vision of violence doesn't aim at clearing the person who ends up committing violent actions, nor does it aim at unburdening that person of all responsibility, or turning that person into a victim. It aims at broadening our understanding of things, and of the levels of responsibility that are superimposed. But the wrongdoer, the criminal, keeps the responsibility of his action. Any person who has had an unhappy childhood, submitted to abuse or violence, doesn't *necessarily* become violent himself (and it's often even the contrary). Our individual choices and responsibility remain. This new way of seeing things – which is not limited to appearances only – reveals all the same a collective responsibility. Through the thoughts and feelings that we harbour, we can, unknowingly, feed the stock – or the cloud – with violence, and those who really commit it can draw from it.

Some people said (and even a play was written about it) that if Hitler had been admitted at the Fine Arts school, to which he applied, the world would have been changed. This seems as convincing to me as imagining that it would only take destroying a steeple or felling a tree for lightning not to fall from the stormy cloud that hovers above our heads. In the transpersonal vision I am developing here, it's obvious that a huge cloud of hatred and violence was hanging over Europe at the time, fuelled by the years of unfortunate choices made after the First World War. Without Hitler, the same load would have found other channels of expression, just like without a high steeple or a tree, lightning strikes the person unconsciously walking in the open in a field, or any other target offering the closest path to the ground. Reducing the Second World War to the influence of a single man is missing a lot of what happened at the time in Europe. It neglects to see how everything took part collectively in building up this load of tension and violence in the cloud throughout the years; though this does, of course, not minimize Hitler's specific role.

The same reasoning can be applied to all kinds of dramatic events nowadays, that we vigorously condemn while reading the paper or watching the news on television, without being aware of the fact that through them, it's maybe a part of our own mental and emotional violence that has found a circumstantial outlet.

But beware! This transpersonal vision is not meant to make us feel guilty: it rather aims at making us take responsibility, making us more aware, and allowing us to make other choices. I will come back to this later, but I must first complete my metaphor.

The Second Cloud

Our little character indeed does not only have occasional murderous thoughts that he doesn't turn into an action. He also happens to have great humanitarian fits, the desire to commit himself to a good cause, to invest in some hope-bringing project. At times, he thinks,

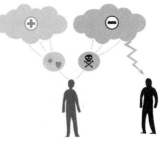

"I'd be happy to work for the *Restos du Coeur*."[14] Or "I'd be happy to go spend a month abroad with an NGO, that takes care of the most destitute, that digs wells, that sets up solar panels, or works at bringing literacy." Or also, "I'd like to commit to the *Colibris*[15] movement, support terminally-ill patients, elderly or handicapped persons, or whatever." But, because of our work, our family, our various obligations, not to forget our fears and doubts, these great feelings and noble intentions often remain virtual ones, and never materialize in our little character's life.

So, what do they become?

---

[14] A French charity that distributes food to the destitute.

[15] A French association based on empowerment, that encourages everyone to do his share to contribute to ecological transition.

You'll never guess: through their similarities, they feed a second cloud, different from the first one, in which, this time, an extraordinary amount of positive energy builds up. And just the same as with the negative cloud, what happens when one, ten, a thousand, a hundred thousand or a million people cherish the same intentions and feelings, without giving them shape in their own life? Well this cloud grows, and grows, and builds up a more and more positive load until . . .

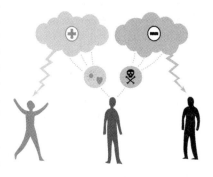

Until it unloads itself, in a different way, through other people be it Mother Teresa, Amma or Gandhi. And these people do exceptional, extraordinary things, they guide, enlighten or heal hundreds of thousands or millions of people. And that's when the world exclaims: "Wow, these are exceptional, wonderful, no ordinary people! They are geniuses, saints, great men or women."

Here again, we can only see the bottom quarter on the left of the drawing: the final result is obvious, visible. It does not occur to us – yet – that maybe, thanks to the remarkable actions of those people, it's in a way part of our own positive intentions, of our own highest feelings and thoughts, that have found their way to take shape and manifest.

What this metaphor of the two clouds suggests is that, we are unknowingly part and parcel of the best and the worst of what happens on this planet: no-one is isolated, cut off from others, 100% autonomous and independent. On the contrary, we are closely linked to one another, we influence one another, to an extent that varies from one individual to another, and mostly depends on our degree of consciousness, therefore on our self-control.

By analogy, in the human body, no cell is totally separated from the others. What's going on in the liver has an influence on the colon as well as the brain. An illness that breaks out in one organ may have come from the saturation or imbalance of another. The slightest cell in the body is therefore influenced by all of the exchanges taking place in the body. That's why symptomatic treatments are not very efficient, because they are limited to what is visible, to the outbreak: sooner or later, the illness will reappear, all the more virulent as its true causes were ignored. Conversely, the so-called holistic medicine, takes into account the individual, not only all of his body in fact, but also his diet, his physical activity, and also his emotional and psychological well-being.

As *cells* of a social body, we too are immersed in a collective atmosphere: on the one hand, we influence it depending on what we are capable of, through the feelings and thoughts that we nourish and that strengthen one cloud or the other. On the other hand, we are also influenced by it, depending on the degree of receptiveness we have towards one mental or emotional frequency, from the highest to lowest ones.

What's interesting in this transpersonal vision of our interactions with one another, as I said above, is that it then allows us to make conscious choices, if we want to.

- What cloud do I feel like feeding, symbolically speaking?

- Will I unconsciously let my mind and my heart chew over any kind of thought or feeling, like wild monkeys, even if it means unconsciously feeding the negative cloud, and then lamenting the flashes of lightning that will inevitably randomly strike here or there?

- Or will I rather consciously tame these two wonderful tools that are at my disposal, my mind and my heart, to direct my thoughts and feelings more and more towards what really matters for me, towards what is bright, positive, and constructive?

Today, there are a considerable number of books and workshops whose goals are to help those people who want to implement inner transformation, to tame their mind and their heart, to turn them into truly conscious allies instead of unconscious saboteurs.[16]

"*What kind of messenger are you?*" is a question that don Miguel Ruiz has, for several years, regularly asked his audience at the end of his lectures. Through what we are, what we say, or what we think, through the feelings and emotions we experience, we keep on sending out messages around us, as if we were radiating light or emitting fragrances. Our look, our posture, the tone of our voice, our body language: everything is language, everything is a message.

And what is this message?

Have we chosen it consciously, deliberately? Or is it the result of our habits, our conditioning, our background, the involuntary and unconscious repetition of something that, actually, does not match our values? Does our everyday presence send out messages of trust, light, hope, love, enthusiasm, sharing, cooperation, or, out of ignorance or unconsciousness, does it rather send out messages that are greyer, darker, heavier, sadder?

Miguel Ruiz asks his audience this question to bring them a sense of awareness and of responsibility: guilt has nothing to do here. The goal is to become aware of our own power, to use it in the way closest to our main values.

The Two Clouds, Morphic Fields, and the Cloud

The metaphor of the two clouds may seem somewhat obscure, New Age, or not very rational to some people. Yet, what I am describing here, with the help of some imagery, actually closely corresponds to the notion of "morphic field" developed for some thirty years by Rupert Sheldrake, whose books I truly recommend reading, in particular the first one *A New Science of Life*.[17]

---

[16] In my book, *J'arrête de (me) juger* (Eyrolles 2014), I compiled more than fifteen different tools, gleaned here and there, that I have used myself to great profit to transform the nature of my thoughts and feelings in my everyday life.

[17] Rupert Sheldrake, *A New Science of Life: The Hypothesis of Formative Causation* (J. P. Tarcher, 1981).

Sheldrake explains that for each form of life there is a "morphic field" – which would have been called an "egregore" in past spiritual circles – that is to say an energetic field. Every crystal, vegetable species or animal has its morphic field. There is a morphic field for human beings. But this goes even farther: every family has its own morphic field, every religion and culture too.

The life experiences of every member of the same species, family or group, feed their corresponding morphic field. And conversely, as a result, this field influences all the individuals linked to it. Here are two examples that will help you understand the principle: the first one focuses on rats, and the second one on human beings.

1. In a lab in Paris, rats have to find their way through a maze to get out of it and be able to eat. At first, they take a long time finding the exit. Then, with some training, they manage to find it within thirty seconds. The same experiment is made again, in New York, with rats from another stock, that had no contact whatsoever with their French counterparts. And what happens is that from the very beginning, the New York rats find the exit practically as quickly as the French ones. In other words, the experience made by the French rats had fed the morphic field – or cloud – of rats, and the information stored in this field then allowed the American rats to immediately match the performances of their European counterparts.

2. In Great Britain, a highly valued crossword puzzle is published every weekend in the Times. This time the experiment consisted in selecting the 20 best crossword experts and to divide them up, randomly, into two groups of 10. The first ten were invited to do the crossword puzzle before it was published in the Times, thus before everybody else. They were timed, and their average time to finish it was noted. Then the Times published its crossword puzzle, and tens of thousands of Brits did it during the weekend while the last 10 crossword experts were kept away. In the end, a few days after all these people had done their crossword puzzle at leisure at home, these last ten people were given it too and were timed. The result? They did it in half the time it took the first ten to do it!

This suggests again that the experience of thousands of Brits had enriched the morphic field that allowed the last ten experts in crosswords to give a beating to their expert counterparts.

Sheldrake, in his various books, introduces dozens of other examples that focus on minerals, as well as vegetables, or human beings, families, societies, and even alphabets! His theory, though not scientifically proven (the energy of these morphic fields remains unknown to this day) but not invalidated either, has been taken up in many subjects from geology, to botany, to psychology and sociology. It provides us with a fascinating theoretical basis for this transpersonal dimension of life which may, tomorrow, undoubtedly become obvious for everybody. And it will considerably change our understanding of interactions and of the level of responsibility that we share with one another, for best or worst, depending on the clouds – the morphic fields – that we choose to feed every day.

Beyond Sheldrake's convergence with morphic fields, and having used this metaphor of the two clouds for a certain number of years already, I have been struck by the emergence of the notion of "Cloud" that has appeared in the past few years in computer science. In this field, the word "Cloud" refers to the place where we can store our data at a distance – files, music, photos, etc. – *through* an Internet connection. Instead of storing everything on our own hard disk, on USB keys, or on backup disks – with the risk of their being stolen, lost or destroyed – the idea is to store our data "in clouds", in immaterial form, from which we can retrieve them at any time, wherever we are on Earth, and on any computer.

In reality of course, the *Cloud* is not immaterial: it's *data centres* in the USA or in Europe, are tremendous premises where there are real hardware computers in which our data is stored at a distance. The only immaterial thing is the Internet connection through which our data is then transferred from our own hard drive to the Cloud from which we can retrieve it later, on any computer.

All the same, the choice of the word *cloud* really reveals something for me, symbolically speaking. In its way, and in its lexical field, it underlines this ongoing evolution that's making us aware of the fact that our world is not merely material – as materialistic scientists wanted us to believe – but that it's also made of imperceptible energies, some of which are still undetectable with the instruments we have today. The numerous experiments of Sheldrake and others, however, continuously prove their reality and very concrete influence.

Clouds and Forgiveness

In obstacle #9 - *Seeing only the personal dimension of the action* – I underlined how difficult it is to implement forgiveness when we not only identify the person with the action committed, but can only see *that* person – as we would only see the trunk of a single tree – without taking into account everything that person is related to, symbolically speaking, his roots and branches. This is just like seeing only the fourth and last quadrant in the metaphor of the two clouds, in the bottom right hand corner: the action itself (see p. 142). And this means that we are deluded by the idea of being isolated, cut off from one another, and that whatever we each go through is independent from what others are experiencing. In our modern world, being so connected through means of communication based on waves, that link us all in invisible ways, and weave between us a lively web of permanent exchanges, supporting the myth of separation becomes paradoxical, if not grotesque.

Bearing these two clouds in mind, and the way we can each contribute to feeding one or the other, we can reach a broadened vision of the wrong suffered, thus widening the channels through which forgiveness can make its way within us. Beyond the specific person that hurt us, this metaphor can in fact help us perceive the whole cycle of violence rather than its mere visible part, and help us to not be limited to the strike of lightning that hit us but to remember also the collective part it takes in the cloud it sprang from.[18]

When I see the person who wronged me as the sole and unique person responsible for his violence, or instead take into account his family background and social sphere, the various influences and

---

[18] I would like to repeat that this metaphor neither excuses nor absolves the person who has done wrong: it only superimposes on that person's own full responsibility another level of collective co-responsibility, depending on the "clouds" we chose to feed or not.

currents that go through him, the morphic fields and clouds he is linked to, it does not infer the same understanding, and does not arouse the same feelings and reactions in me. As has often been expressed throughout these pages, forgiveness is not only a matter of heart and good feelings, it's also closely linked to the way we see and understand the situation: the more narrow-minded we are, the more limited are the paths to forgiveness. Conversely, the wider our comprehension, the larger and more open are the channels through which the water of forgiveness may flow within us.

It's also a lesson in humility that these two clouds give us, in a certain way, at a time when, on the contrary, some American New Age trends would like to make us believe in a kind of mighty power and total control over our own reality. Humility, indeed, for these clouds underline that in fact my fate is unfailingly linked to that of the others. I can make all possible efforts in my own little corner to live well, to become better, to be faithful to certain ideals and values, but I am also dependent on the social circle I move around in, and I'm not the only one to decide on which clouds will fly over a certain time and culture, even if I can attempt, with others, to push them one way or another.

We live in a world shaped, from one second to another, by what millions, or billions of people think, feel and desire. So the need for humility, to accept the world as it is and our specific place in it. Humility is a tremendous antidote to our judgements, as much those we promptly make against ourselves as those we so quickly utter against other people, especially the ones who have wronged us. It puts us back on equal footing with one another, far from the haughty pretentions of our mind in its ivory tower. It allows to sometimes act without being a control-freak, sometimes to accept without resigning ourself. And when necessary, it makes the path to forgiveness a lot easier.

Last but not least, this metaphor of the two clouds – and the quick outline I drew here of Sheldrake's morphic fields – highlights a crucial point: nothing we do, even alone at home, even lost in the wilderness of mountains or desert, remains without effect. Each one of our thoughts and intentions, each one of our feelings, but also every one of our regular practices, feed, through affinity, the corresponding cloud or morphic field. Which means that on the one hand we help other people to think, love and act in the same way as us, and on the other hand that we, in turn, are helped and supported in our efforts, by all of those who have made the choice to go the same way as us. Physically, yes, we each have a different body, we seem isolated from one another. But on psychological, energetic and spiritual levels, no-one is alone, we are permanently linked to one another, and thus we create "families", groups of people who support and mutually reinforce one another from a distance without even knowing it, in what we learn and how fulfilled we are.

So, now, it's up to you to choose which fields and which clouds you will from now on develop!

Recommended Reading

Clerc, Olivier. *The Gift of Forgiveness*. Forres, UK: Findhorn Press, 2010.

Fisher, Robert. *The Knight in Rusty Armour*. Chatsworth, CA: Wilshire Book Company, 1987.

Grof, Stanislav. *When the Impossible Happens: Adventures in Non Ordinary Realities*. Boulder, CO: Sounds True, 1st edition, 2006.

Luskin, Fred. *Forgive for Good: A Proven Prescription for Health and Happiness*. New York: HarperOne, revised edition, 2003.

Pennac, Daniel. *School Blues*. London, UK: Quercus Publishing, 2011.

Ruiz, Miguel. *Beyond Fear: A Toltec Guide to Freedom and Joy*. Chicago, IL: Council Oak Books, 1st edition, 1997.

Sheldrake, Rupert. *A New Science of Life: The Hypothesis of Formative Causation*. London, UK: Icon Books, 2009.

Tipping, Colin. *Radical Forgiveness: A Revolutionary Five-Stage Process to Heal Relationships, Let Go of Anger and Blame, and Find Peace in Any Situation*. Boulder, CO: Sounds True, 2010.

The Forgiveness Project

The *Forgiveness Project* is a British charity founded by the British journalist Marina Cantacuzino. It relies on the genuine stories of people who have committed or survived violence, to explore the concept of forgiveness, and alternatives to revenge. It is offered in prisons, schools, companies, and local communities, as well as with anyone who wants to examine the nature of forgiveness, whether in their own life, or within a larger political context.

The *Forgiveness Project* set up an exceptional exhibition, The "F" Word, gathering the worldwide testimonies of people who often experienced terrible traumas, and who were then able to implement forgiveness. This exhibition travelled throughout the United Kingdom and to many other countries. It can be found on the website of the *Forgiveness Project*.

For the first gathering of the *Days of Forgiveness* at the *Val de Consolation* in 2012, I was granted permission to translate about a dozen of these stories into French, and to exhibit them on big printed boards. Beyond this material exhibition, my wish was to enable them to be as widely read as possible, and I thank Marina Cantacuzino for having allowed me to print some of these stories in this book.

Teaching forgiveness becomes meaningful throughout these stories. They show that one can be cured of the unspeakable.

For more information, see:

theforgivenessproject.com

Acknowledgments

My heartfelt thanks to Marina Cantacuzino, founder of the *Forgiveness Project* in London, for having allowed me to add several accounts of people having experienced forgiveness, and to whom I would also like to express my deep gratitude: Andrew Rice, Yulie Cohen, Bud Welch, Katy Hutchison & Ryan Aldridge, Mary Foley, Ginn Fourie and Letlapa Mphahlele.

Thank you also to Dr Fred Luskin and to Colin Tipping for having allowed me to introduce their respective approaches to forgiveness.

And last, but not least, my thanks go to those who took part in my workshops, and who took the trouble to share their experience with me. Some of their testimonies are scattered here and there in the following pages: Sylvie, Mylène, Patrick, Véronique, Dominique, Laure, and Thomas.

Index

Index

Index

About the Author

Photo by Patrick Gaillardin

For more than thirty years, **Olivier Clerc** has been blending his personal progression of spirituality and self-help with a professional career as an author, lecturer, and trainer. Of Swiss origin and now living in France, he has published some twenty-five books, with translations in seventeen languages, including *The Gift of Forgiveness: A Magical Encounter with Don Miguel Ruiz*, first published in 2010.

The practice of the Gift of Forgiveness is a transpersonal tool that, when experienced in a group, allows a person to express and receive forgiveness even from people who are not physically present to take part. It doesn't require any prior knowledge and can be practiced by anyone.

To satisfy the growing demand for heart healing that forgiveness brings, Olivier decided he needed to train people to lead autonomous Forgiveness Circles. In 2012, he founded the Association Pardon International (API), and he and his workshop leaders have trained 700 people to create Circles of Forgiveness worldwide. There are now more than 300 of these in 15 countries around the world. Olivier is also the creator of the International Forgiveness Day, celebrated all over the world every year on the 18th of September.

www.olivierclerc.com

Also by Olivier Clerc

The Gift of Forgiveness

A Magical Encounter with don Miguel Ruiz

Drawn from a Toltec workshop with don Miguel Ruiz, the author unearths and explores the unique and simple tool of forgiveness and shows how it brings immediate relief and unleashes the love blocked by personal resentments. Through the magic of reversal taught in this guide, readers can change their understanding of forgiveness and free themselves from the grip of resentments and hatred.

ISBN 9-781-84409-190-4

Also of Interest

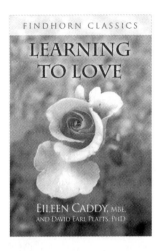

Learning to Love

Eileen Caddy, MBE, and David Earl Platts, Ph.D

This insightful guide shows ways to explore feelings, attitudes, and past experiences that block you from loving and receiving love. Drawing from Roberto Assagioli's system of psychosynthesis, they include exercises, meditations, and visualizations to support you in examining your inner world and implementing acceptance, trust, forgiveness, and risk-taking, to bring more harmony and joy to your life.

ISBN 9–781–62055–835–5

FINDHORN PRESS

Life-Changing Books

Learn more about us and our books at
www.findhornpress.com

For information on the Findhorn Foundation:
www.findhorn.org